MW01632181

WHAT'S LOVE GOT TO DO WITH IT?...

"Everything," Says Jesus

William H. Aulenbach

ISBN 0-7414-4781-9

Published by:

1094 New DeHaven Street, Suite 100
West Conshohocken, PA 19428-2713
Info@buybooksontheweb.com
www.buybooksontheweb.com
Toll-free (877) BUY BOOK
Local Phone (610) 941-9999
Fax (610) 941-9959

Printed in the United States of America

Printed on Recycled Paper

Published July 2008

What's Love Got To Do With It?… "Everything," Says Jesus

is dedicated to my wife Anne…
My best friend since 1960…
Mother of Gretchen, Heidi and Alison…
Wonderful grandmother to Ryan, Trevor, Kaya and Molly.
Thanks Annie for being a lover.

Acknowledgments

One doesn't write a book without help of many others people. My book is no exception and I would like to offer my special thanks to:

- St. Mary's Episcopal Church, Laguna Beach, California for allowing me to lecture on the content of my book to start to work out the kinks.
- Good friends Jackie and Darryl Marshall, Dee Mahuna, Ron Clyde and Barbara Skopeck who took time from their busy lives to reviews the early drafts.
- Tammy Olson, Richard Hille and my Anne for reviewed the book twice. All your suggestions were fantastic and helped me pull the book together.
- My sister-in-law, Dege Donati, an artist and great human being who designed the cover. I very much appreciate all her creativity and hard work. I can't forget her husband John who offered great advice and support.
- Another friend, Chris Russell, was a reviewer, typist and editor. Chris also was a great help with my previous book, ***How To Get To Heaven Without Going to Church.***
- Tammy Olson also doubled as an editor who dotted all the "i"s and crossed all the "t"s, amidst her very full life.
- Our daughter Alison Barrett who gave me some great marketing ideas.
- Cristina Calderone who did the final editing before the book was sent to the publisher.

It "takes a village" to write a book and I am most appreciative to my "village" for all their support and hard work.

CONTENTS

"Love and do as you please."
Saint Augustine, *On the Epistle of John 7*

INTRODUCTION

My almost fifty years of ministry as an Episcopal priest has been diversified, different and, at times difficult. This is primarily because I have the tendency to think outside the box about life and especially about the Christian faith, so much so, that occasionally people will ask me if I truly consider myself a Christian. Quickly I respond that there is absolutely no question in my mind that I am a Christian. Jesus is my Christ - which for me is the primary requisite for calling oneself a Christian. However, I am quick to add, perhaps I am not a very good Episcopalian because I do not always subscribe to some of their creeds and basic theology. For example, about two thirds of both the ancient Nicene and Apostles' creeds do not relate to me in the 21st century. The mythical image of who they claim Jesus was does not make sense to me; i.e., "born of a Virgin." "His (God's) only Son," "descended to the dead…rose again…ascended into heaven," "is seated at the right hand of the Father." "He will come again to judge the living and the dead." I know that I am not alone in thinking this way. There are even people within the church who keep their fingers crossed when they recite the creeds.

I believe that the present direction of so many of the mainstream American churches (those that have been around for 100 or more years) is self-destructive. As a result their membership numbers are rapidly declining. They seem to be closing far more churches than they are opening.

However, I feel strongly that if these churches were to make some radical changes they could reverse this trend. In my estimation, one of the more important changes they need to make is to espouse completely the ethics of Jesus. I think Jesus' main mission to his own Jewish people was to bring them back to the concept of love - of self, neighbor and God.

I went to seminary (1957 to 1960) at The Church Divinity School of the Pacific (CDSP) located in Berkeley, California, a town known for its liberal ways. CDSP also had a reputation for being open and progressive. It was ingrained into my thinking that Christians need to be open to new ideas, be continually growing in the faith and that one's theology can never be stagnant. It must change with the times. This is challenging in today's rather quickly changing world. I encourage others to continually rethink their faith and to make certain that their theology works for them on a daily basis.

When teaching, one of my favorite exercises is to find out the thinking of the people involved, so I ask them to share with me their ideas about God, Jesus and the Holy Spirit. Their responses run the gamut from ultra conservative to very progressive. Some people have stock answers from ***The Book of Common Prayer*** and its 'The Catechism' (***Book of Common Prayer*** page 852); others give answers they had learned in Sunday school. A few admit they aren't sure. Their responses to who is God and who was/is Jesus, for the most part, are what they have been taught to believe. Very few people have a reply to, "Who is the Holy Spirit?" This concept baffles many, for good reasons.

About fifteen years ago I added a fourth question having to do with Christian ethics. I would inquire, "What is the foundation of Christian ethics?" It was almost like asking, "Who is the Holy Spirit?" Primarily, I would receive blank stares. Someone might then ask, "What do you mean by ethic?" So I would try again. "What is the ethical/moral standard by which Christians need to make moral/ethical decisions?" There would be a few guesses "The Ten Commandments." "The Beatitudes!" "The Bible?" "Jesus?" "What 'Father' (clergy) tells me to do!" More often than not I would receive blank stares. Occasionally someone would say, "The Great Commandment" or maybe even "Love". This surprised me because too many Christians do not understand what the basic message of Jesus is.

None of these questions were an attempt to make people feel foolish. I was simply gathering information. Answers to the first three questions resulted in my writing a book entitled, ***How to Get To Heaven Without Going to Church***. In that book I tried to share, in a simplistic way, what I felt would be a theology that would be attractive to progressive thinkers willing to look at a new way of approaching Christianity. In spite of the title, which some people interpreted as heresy, the book had quite the opposite effect. The line of thinking in that book did make sense to some within the church and many of those either on the periphery or outside. Readers appreciated the fact that clergy in the church were questioning some of the same things they were.

However, in that book, I did not address Christian ethics. It was too big a subject and I did not want to make it a tome. My belief is that Christianity is a rather simple way of life and one does not need to read volumes in order to understand it. Perhaps one of the reasons why so many Christians don't really comprehend their religion is that they perceive it as complex and believe that only those who study it for years can start to fathom what it is to be one. I disagree with that idea because I believe that Jesus was a human being with an extraordinary message that is not at all difficult to comprehend. To me, he was a radical revolutionary whose revolution was all about love.

I believe this inaccurate portrayal is also a reflection on the institutional church. (When I refer to the institutional church, I mean those churches that have a hierarchy no matter how small or large. They usually have buildings, rules, take monetary collections and are a business.) They seem to be much more interested in the "Sermon on the Amount," than the "Sermon on the Mount." In so many Episcopal churches there is minimal teaching. From my perspective, the preaching in the Episcopal Church can be horrendous. In my seminary experience, we were not taught how to preach. Perhaps there was a homiletics (preaching) course or two in a three-year seminary experience but that was the extent of it for developing preachers. There seems to be a great deal more emphasis on ***The Book of Common Prayer*** and the liturgy than on developing the art of preaching and teaching.

As in ***How to Get to Heaven Without Going to Church***, I have written this book in an attempt to give readers a simple concise answer as to what I see is the basic ethical standard for Christians. It is not complicated. My biggest challenge is to share what it isn't and then to teach how to apply the ethic of Jesus to everyday living. Jesus and scripture are very clear about this ethic. Although the ethical issue might be complex, our basic Christian response ought always to be the same - to love.

Using Jesus' ethical approach to decision making has changed my life dramatically. It took a few years of being in the ministry before I caught on and I give a great deal of credit to a fellow Episcopal priest who was, at one time, the Dean of an Episcopal cathedral and then taught ethics at the Episcopal seminary in Cambridge, Massachusetts. His name, Joseph Fletcher, is still famous, or notorious, depending upon one's point of view. His book ***Situation Ethics: The New Morality*** was first published in 1966. For me, he really clarified the issue. For others, some of whom might not even have read the book, Fletcher was a heretic and a psycho-ceramic (a crackpot).

In his first chapter he tells a joke, which I have repeated numerous times. It's fun and has a message: An older rich man asked a lovely young lady if she would spend the night with him. She said, "No." He then asked her if she would do it for $100,000. She said, "Yes." He then asked if she would do it for $10,000. She had to think about that for a few moments and then replied, "Well…yes." His next question was "How about $50?" She was furious. "What do you think I am?" He responded, "We've already established that. Now we're haggling over the price."

The message for me: Jesus gave us an ethic by which to live. That has been well established. The institutional church seems to me to be constantly haggling over how to put his ethics into practice.

One of the more widespread ideas in the Christian community is that the Ten Commandments are the ethics of Jesus and therefore the basis of Christianity. When one tells those who espouse this concept that the Ten Commandments are the Old Testament and Christians are about the New Testament, one is often met with a blank stare. Then try to suggest that Christians really don't follow the Ten Commandments. They just think they do. (How many Christians keep holy the Sabbath - Saturdays?)

There is also the misconception that God wrote the Scriptures. So many have the image of an old man, sitting "up there", writing each book of the Bible in the order in which they are found in the King James Version. Of course, he wrote using King James English. He crossed every "t," dotted every "i," and then said, "This is it…forever and ever. There will be no more additions or deletions." Next, he threw it down to earth. (We're not exactly sure of that date.) And here it is. God help the person who tries to study it with an investigative eye or who might suggest it has contradictions, inconsistencies and misinformation. They will be dismissed, literally and figuratively. With such a fundamental approach, it is almost impossible to understand the ethics of Jesus.

This leads to the next problem. Many like to quote from selected passages of Scripture, often taken out of context, to support their biases. If the Bible says it (regardless of the circumstances under which it was said), then it has to be true. One of the favorites these days comes from those who love to quote Scripture whenever it might suggest something derogatory about people with a different sexual orientation. They quote primarily from the Old Testament, even though Christianity is about the New Testament. Concerning homosexuality, these same people will then claim that the Bible is the ultimate authority. But these same folks seem to conveniently ignore the fact that according to the Old Testament Book of Leviticus, "believers" are also not to eat pork (bacon, spareribs and pigs feet) nor shellfish (crabs, lobsters or shrimp), engage in sex during a woman's menstruation or have a medium rare camel steak. (This last prohibition is not a big problem for most folks I know.) I do not understand why Biblical literalists don't rally against these other prohibitions? I have yet to see a sign that reads, "God Hates People Who Eat Pork, Lobster, Shrimp and Camel Steaks! And Women Who Have Sex During Menstruation!" Could it be that they simply pick and choose the passages that support their prejudices? My contention is that if followers understood the ethics of Jesus, these so-called issues would become non-issues.

This feeds into the next problem: People love the law. It doesn't seem to make any difference that Jesus came to save us from the law, "You shall love the Lord your God with all your heart, and with all your soul and with all your mind. This is the first and great commandment. And a second is like it, you shall love your neighbor as yourself. *On these two commandments depend all the law and the prophets*"(Matthew 22:37). Mark 12:31 says the above but concludes, "There is no other commandment greater than these." Luke 10:25 reiterates and states, "Do this and you shall live." Nor do many understand that Christianity was built along the idea of individual freedom and responsibility. That is too scary for many folks and immediately they will revert to the law, because life is easier if one follows the law rather than make a decision based on the situation and love.

I think the perception by so many people of who Jesus is presents a problem. I call it "My Sweet Jesus" image. He was so nice to everyone. He never said an unkind word or had a nasty thought. Sexually, he was neutered. He would never start an argument, put someone down, tell someone off or insult another. Of course, he was a pacifist. He appeared a little emaciated, was a 97 pound weakling, had a perfectly coiffed hairdo (pageboy style), pink skin, clean fingernails and walked/swished about two inches off the ground.

Unfortunately, this “My Sweet Jesus” image is portrayed as such by too many artists, poets, and hymn writers. (In my childhood church there was a painted portrait over one of the altars that depicted Jesus this way.)

Why do people have so many problems seeing Jesus as a radical revolutionary, an agitator, an opinionated teacher who told it like it was, in no uncertain terms? As someone once said, “They didn’t put Jesus on a cross because he said, ‘Consider the lilies of the field and how they grow.’ (Matthew 6:28) but rather because he said, look at the Pharisees and how rotten they are!” A “My Sweet Jesus” portrayal makes absolutely no sense. However, his radical revolutionary image was and still is revolutionizing the world.

Semantics are also a part of the problem. The institutional church loves to throw words around such as ethics, morality, love, forgiveness and a long list of other terms. Unfortunately, the church doesn’t often define these terms and as a result we seem to be using the same words, but with different meanings. The word love is a good example. People use this word to talk about how they feel about their pet, spouse, children, car, food and so forth. But what do they really mean when they use that word? How intense are their feelings? What does it include? The ethics of Jesus does not have a semantics problem. The definition of his message is very clear.

Then there are the Christian slogans that confuse the issue. Believers love to fling around little sayings, especially on bumpers. “Honk if you love Jesus.” “God Loves You!” “He died for your sins!” “You are forgiven!” “WWJD” (“What Would Jesus Do?”) One of my favorites is, “Look busy! Jesus is coming.” The one Christian slogan/phrase that always peaks my interest is the one which states, “I believe in Traditional Family Values.” This phrase does not make any sense to me. Its proponents suggest that the man is the head of the household. The “little wife” is subservient and the children are little soldiers who do as the Master of the house tells them. It implies that if one does life this way, then everyone will live happily thereafter. I have no idea where they get these ideas (perhaps from the bachelor Paul), but they certainly do not come from the life of Jesus, a man constantly at odds with his family. His siblings and perhaps his mother thought Jesus was strange and, at one point, were even willing to allow others to stone him to death. For most of his adult life, Jesus had little to do with them. Just looking at his own lifestyle, I believe the ethics of Jesus challenges such erroneous thinking as "Traditional Family Values."

Another mantra I hear over and over in some form goes like this: America's values are in the toilet and a clogged one at that. Granted the media helps to generate this concept because bad news, gossip and crime sell a lot more papers, movies and TV shows. But in my little world of friends, acquaintances, and neighbors I find good people trying to live a sensible lifestyle, whether they are Christians or not. I do not see the values of this great country dissipating. I see them changing rapidly as have our lives over the past 100 years. Unfortunately, I do not see the institutional church keeping up with the changes. As a consequence, many religious institutions still operate from values established a very long time ago in a very different world. However, the ethics of Jesus will always remain relevant, even in a fast - changing world.

In my years in the business as a professional (and the church is BIG business) I have not found many clergy who openly espouse the ethics of Jesus and use it as a constant theme in their preaching and teaching. I am not certain why they openly avoid the subject, but it could be that they do not really understand Jesus' ethics. Maybe they are too busy with "The Sermon on the Amount" or running their "franchise" to make certain that each member of their flock understands how to live the ethics of Jesus. My theory is that there would be fewer problems in the institutional church if his ethics were understood and used on a daily basis.

With this information in mind I have felt the need to present the ethics of Jesus in a book form. I have taught it in classes, received feedback and now want to share my findings based on years of experience, listening and studying. Some will find my ideas offensive and insulting. Others will be comfortable with my way of thinking. Whatever your feelings are, I would ask that you keep an open mind. As you will discover as I share with you my journey in the faith, it has not always been easy to arrive at some of my beliefs. I can assure you that the learning curve is still going on and changes are continually being made. As you read this book, I hope that you too will examine your own ethical system, make corrections where needed and continue to grow "in wisdom and in stature, and in favor with God and man" (Luke 2:52).

In writing this book, I have attempted to present to the reader a systematic approach. Each chapter will be built on the foundation I have laid in the previous chapter. This methodology starts in Chapter 1, "Confusion Reigns," where I share with you some of my faith journey since I was five years old. I talk about some of the important moral and ethical issues of our times, some of which have been baffling to me and perhaps to you also.

Chapter 2, "Theologically Speaking..." gives the reader a brief summary of my theology. I hope this will help so that when I use a word, you will have an understanding what it means to me. Some might see my theology as different, maybe even heretical, but I have been wrestling with it for years - and continue to do so.

In the next chapter, "What Jesus' Ethics Aren't," I shall share with you what I believe are *not* the ethics of Jesus. Unfortunately, too many Christians subscribe to one or more of these principles. As a result, it could be difficult to understand clearly just what the ethics of Jesus are.

Chapter 4 deals with "The Ethics of Jesus." I think these are spelled out very clearly in Scripture. I shall deal with some background information and then present the essence of this book.

What do I mean when I speak of ethics, morality, values, love, forgiveness and acceptance? Some of them, especially love, take a great deal of explanation. So that we all have a mutual understanding, in Chapter 5, "Let's Define Terms," I do just that.

The sixth chapter is entitled, "Jesus and His Friends Talk About Love." Here I try to show the many ways Jesus explained his ethics and how his followers picked up on his primary message.

Chapter 7 will be, "Putting the Ethics of Jesus into Action." We have this beautiful ethic, but how does one make it work in our daily experiences and challenges?

Chapter 8 is entitled, "What Would You Do?" We shall take a look at ten specific ethical challenges and actually make some theoretical decisions based on the information we have been given. It is not always easy to come up with clear-cut answers.

The final Chapter, "The Challenges Ahead," will discuss what it is that we need to do in order to put our words and thinking into action, especially in our daily living.

I hope you enjoy this book and that it makes you think about your own system for making ethical/moral decisions. It would be my deepest hope that the ethics of Jesus will help you to be a better person and to make this a better world in which to live.

Peace Love Joy
William (Bil) Aulenbach

All Scriptural passages quoted are from either the Revised Standard Version or the New Revised Standard Version.

"Do not think that I have come to bring peace on earth. I have not come to bring peace, but a sword." Matthew 10:34

CHAPTER 1

"CONFUSION REIGNS"

A boy got on the bus and sat next to a man reading a book and noticed that he had his collar on backwards. He stared at the man for a few minutes and then asked him why he wore his collar backwards.

The man, who was a priest, said, "I am a Father."

The little boy replied, "My Dad's a father and he doesn't wear his collar backwards."

The priest looked down from his book and said, "I am the Father of many."

The lad said, "My Dad has four boys, four girls and two grandchildren and he still doesn't wear his collar backwards.

The priest, becoming a bit impatient, replied, "I am the Father of hundreds." and went back to reading his book.

The boy sat quietly until it was time for him to get off the bus. As he got up he leaned over to the priest and said, "Well, sir, maybe instead of wearing your collar backwards, you should try wearing your pants backwards!"

Does the quotation from Matthew at the top of the page confuse you? I find it confusing in light of the stereotype of Jesus as a pacifist. Then there is the confusion in the joke of the boy when he tried to get an explanation from the priest as to why he wore his collar backwards. (Why *do* clergy wear those miserable uncomfortable collars?) During my years of being a professional in the church, I have found so many of the issues surrounding ethics and morality as presented by the institutional church, most confusing. Let me be more specific and share with you some of my journey in the faith.

The church was very much a part of my life from day one. My Dad was an Episcopal clergyman and, to most people, a very successful one. He was outspoken, colorful, controversial, stood up to authority, an excellent preacher and had standing room only in his church. The ministry was his life.

At the age of five my favorite game was "church," which consisted of mimicking what happened on Sundays. In the sixth grade I went to The Episcopal Academy, a boys' preparatory school founded in 1785. At first I had two sets of friends, one from church and one from school. As girls came into our lives the two became one. Many of my female church friends dated my prep school buddies. I became an acolyte, a very prestigious position in our church, demanding weekly training on a Friday evening. I was involved in the church youth group. My girlfriend went to my Dad's church. I went to church two or three times on Sunday as well as every day at school. Although I disliked Sunday school, I did have good religious training at my prep school. My primary punishment for my sins of omission and/or commission was ***not*** being allowed to go to Sunday evening church. That's different because most teenagers would not see that as punishment. In fact, I was attracted to the ministry, but I never told anyone because I was afraid I would be ostracized as a goody goody.

I went to an Episcopal college, Kenyon College in Gambier, Ohio. However, sports, fraternity life and beer seemed to overpower my religious life. Underneath the facade of college life I still felt religious, but I made certain no one else saw it. It was the Korean War and, as graduation loomed near, I felt a pull, go to seminary or into the service. My lacrosse coach had been a Marine during World War II. He was a man I greatly admired and he convinced me that a stint in the Corps would make me a leader of men and give me time to figure out what I was going to do with the rest of my life.

Eight weeks after graduating from Kenyon, I was in Marine Corps boot camp in Quantico, Virginia. I went from being a BMOC ("big man on campus") to the lowliest of human beings. This was one of the more difficult experiences in my life not only because the Marines have a way of making this happen, but also because I made a terrible faux pas. Because my name starts with "A", I was one of the first in my platoon to lead the platoon in marching. I had no idea what I was doing. Accidentally I marched them into a chain link fence. After the platoon sergeant "picked" the men out of the fence and put them back in formation, he came to me (I was standing at rigid attention, dead serious, staring straight ahead), put his face about six inches from my face, stared in my eyes a few moments and then screamed, "Aulenbach, you ain't got no more brains than an ant!" At that moment, I thought it was very funny and I laughed. Some of the other men in the platoon did also. This was a second terrible mistake. The platoon sergeant thought I was laughing at him and not with him. From that day forward, his mission was to wash me out of the Corps. On a daily basis, he made my life miserable. Every Saturday he failed me and sent me before a review board. Every Saturday they sent me back to the platoon for another week of misery. But I was determined to persevere.

After eight weeks of this it came down to the final week and a review board. They were to make the final decision as to whether I would be a private or a second lieutenant. This review board consisted of four highly decorated, high-ranking officers who were going to put us through their version of hell. Part way through the four-day test, I felt I was doing well and went out of the barracks in the evening to take a pensive walk, alone. It was dark when I passed by the chapel and something inside me said, "Go inside." I did. I sat down and suddenly this peace came over me. The last eight weeks had been tense. I was now feeling very calm. My mind said, "Bil, no matter what happens, it will work out for you. If you make it and are commissioned, fine. If you don't make it and must remain a private for the next two years, it's going to work. Stay positive and continue to give it your best shot." I sat there for quite awhile feeling very good about myself and my life ahead, whatever it might be.

I call this my conversion experience. There was no question in my mind that Christianity had to be a major part of my life. In two days, I was to find out my future. At the end of the four days of being tested by the officers, I had to appear before them. I thought I had done well, but only those four officers knew my fate. Dressed in my best uniform, rather nervous, I stood at attention. One of them, a Captain with about eight rows of battle ribbons, started working me over. Finally he said, "Aulenbach, you didn't make it. You won't be commissioned. Leave here and report immediately to the office for your orders to your next duty station."

I remember it being a very windy, rainy day, the tail end of a hurricane. As I walked to the office to start my next two years as a private I felt fine, a bit disappointed, but very willing to accept the next challenge. I reported to the office. The phone rang and the clerk asked me, "Are you Aulenbach?" I said, "Yes, Sir." and he told me to report back immediately to the review board. A little fear and trepidation set in, but I went right back. The Captain who had given me "the good news" asked me what I was doing there? I told him I had been ordered to return. He told me to come into the room. He had me stand "at ease" and then said, "Aulenbach, you did very well during the test. We were impressed. The final test was to see if you follow orders well. You did and you'll be commissioned a 2nd Lieutenant in the U.S. Marine Corps on Saturday."

It was good news, great news, but the best news that day was that I knew I had a faith that was going to see me through life. Christianity was to be the foundation of my life no matter what direction it took.

I had an excellent experience in the Corps. It taught me about discipline, leading, life, people and how to deal creatively with constant challenges. However, it was not always easy, even as an officer. I had my fair share of difficult experiences, but now felt I had the tools of my faith to help me move through each of them. I thought my first duty station was to be Korea, but then I received orders to report to Kaneohe Marine Corps Air Station on the island of O'ahu in Hawai'i. Shortly after I arrived I became involved in the Episcopal church and had the opportunity to meet their bishop, The Right Reverend Harry S. Kennedy. One day the Bishop invited me for lunch. In the course of the meal he asked me if I was interested in going into the ministry. I admitted that I had given it serious thought but felt that I was "not ready," which is really a code word meaning "I am not worthy." Or "I am terrified at the thought of having to deal with other people's problems, preaching a different sermon every week, running a parish (big business), being at an altar and performing all the sacraments." Obviously, the Bishop saw me as a potential candidate and left me with these words: "I understand your concerns but if you ever feel that you would like to go to seminary I would be happy to sponsor you." A seed had been planted and was slowly germinating.

I was the Executive Officer of a Motor Transport company for a brigade. I had been promoted to Captain and had received orders to go to the U.S. Naval Academy as the Company commander of the Rifle Range and to help run the Marine Guard stationed there. It was an exciting opportunity. Then along came my call to the ministry, in a very unusual way.

Periodically all Marine Corps units are inspected by outside inspectors to ascertain their readiness. The inspection of my company was to be at 1:30 PM. The troops and vehicles were almost ready, but we were spending the morning doing last minute preparations. After lunch, my men were to get into their inspection uniforms and be all ready by 1 PM. Unfortunately, the inspector misread his time chart and showed up at 11:30 a.m. We were not ready and the inspector said he understood, but then went and reported to the Colonel of the brigade that the Motor Transport outfit was a total mess. The Colonel called me in and started chewing me out. I tried to explain, but he would not listen.

Suddenly, I had my call to the ministry. I interrupted the Colonel and said, “Colonel, I don’t really care about your threats (demotion and transfer) because when you’re finished with your unreasonable tirade I’m leaving this office and getting out of the Marines.” He could not believe it and dismissed me. I went to my office, called the Bishop, told him what happened and said, “I just had my calling to go into the ministry. I now need to have my orders changed and start the process of applying to The Church Divinity School of the Pacific.” The Bishop, having been in Hawai’i since 1942, knew every Marine General stationed in the Pacific basin. He placed his phone calls and within two weeks I had my orders to report to Treasure Island (San Francisco) for discharge and was accepted at CDSP to start seminary in the fall of 1957. As peculiar as the circumstances were, I knew this was the right thing to do. I was ready and maybe even worthy.

Seminary was an unbelievable experience. Along with college and the Marine Corps, I would say seminary was one of my great life changing opportunities. As with most seminarians, there is always this nagging thought, “Am I worthy?” But one is so busy with school, learning, changing, growing that one does not have too much time to dwell on that thought. Also, it was a very interesting time in the life of Christianity. John the 23rd was Pope and he was turning Roman Catholicism upside down. Christians were talking with each other. Different religions were in dialogue. Biblical criticism was recognized. Scholars were searching for the historical Jesus. The antiquated liturgies were being rewritten in the vernacular using modern language. The Church was a power in the world. My own denomination was growing. Many new churches were being built and they were filled with people who were interested in doing mission. Almost half my seminary class was going into the mission field.

I was learning how to be an Episcopal priest. I knew my seminary was on the cutting edge of the “reformation.” I was excited about the future of the church and my role in that future. The three years went very quickly, and in June of 1960, I felt worthy to be ordained a priest in the Episcopal church.

My first job was as an assistant overseeing a youth church comprised of 350 teenagers in a large, lively parish just south of Honolulu. I now had a new learning curve, the reality of the ministry. I had a great boss, a rector who had really dealt with the realities of life. He had been a prisoner of war, captured by the Japanese in the Philippines very early in World War II, and one of the only people in his company who made it out alive. It was at this parish that I met my wife Anne. She was the beautiful new kindergarten teacher fresh out of college. We were married there in June of 1961. Our oldest daughter was born in Honolulu. My first ministry was a great learning experience, and then along came another.

The Dean of the seminary in Strasbourg, France offered me a full scholarship to come to his seminary and start the work on my doctorate. I was encouraged to accept this opportunity. In Strasbourg, I met seminarians from many different denominations from all over the world. The title of my thesis was, "The Influence of the Old Testament on the Gospel of Mark." The premise was that everything Jesus did in that Gospel had either been done or prophesied in the Old Testament. In many circles this was heretical thinking. My tutor suggested that I ***never*** preach or teach about this subject to laity or to most clergy. This sort of thinking was way outside the box and I was part of it. The church became more and more exciting for me.

In September, 1964 we moved from Strasbourg, France to Wailuku, Maui where I became the Rector of a small parish. This was a real cultural shock, but on Maui I found a great group of young clergy from all denominations who were elated about the direction of the church. We did all sorts of outreach work in never-before-seen cooperative ventures. Our second daughter was born. Anne had had problems with the pregnancy and unbeknownst to her she had contracted rubella in the first trimester of her pregnancy. Our daughter was born with multiple challenges and it soon became obvious that we could not meet these challenges if we stayed on Maui. But once more I had that "peace," the one ***The Book of Common Prayer*** calls "the peace that passes all understanding." Armed with the faith that we could deal with any challenge presented, we planned our move. Those of you who have children with special needs understand the immensity of it.

The first parish where I had been now had a new rector. The youth group had dwindled from 350 to about 40 youth. He asked me if I would be interested in returning. He would give me carte blanche to do innovative youth programming, if I would consider it. I really enjoyed working with young people and accepted the challenge. Within two years we had a youth church comprised of some 2,500 teenagers involved in a myriad of activities that obviously made sense to them. We were again on the cutting edge of making the church relevant to young people. The Episcopal church, and even *TIME* magazine in their Religion section, was noticing what was happening.

The war in Vietnam was raging. I was against it, especially seeing so many body bags with dead youth coming home. Young people were dying for a cause no one seemed to fully understand. Our drama group wanted to stage a play called, "Viet Rock," an exposé about the war. This threatened some of the defense contractors in the church. The Rector and I spoke and we decided not to stage it at the church. However, an opportunity came about to put it on at a church where they were holding anti-war rallies. The play went very well. The newspapers picked it up and the next morning at 7 a.m. the Rector sought me out (I was cleaning toilets because my maintenance man had called in sick) and fired me on the spot, for putting on that play. There was no discussion, only threats. I was to have no contact with the youth, perform no pastoral responsibilities in the parish and our family (my wife, three daughters under 7 years of age with the middle one being multi-handicapped) had 30 days to vacate the church-owned house in which we lived.

We were shunned by the members of that church. I called the Bishop at 9 a.m. and told him what had happened. He said, "Fine. I just hired you as the Diocesan Youth Director." That was all well and good, but I could not believe what had just happened. I had "the peace" but I also had a great deal of confusion. Why would a fellow Christian, a brother priest, do such a dastardly thing to me and my family? All I was doing was relating the Good News to youth, speaking my piece about an unjust war and working about 70 hours a week? He refused to talk about it. Is this the Gospel preached by Jesus?

(This is an appendix to my firing: Thirteen years later, after the Rector retired, he sent me a note asking for my forgiveness. He told me he did not fire me for my stance on the Vietnam war. He fired me because the success of the youth congregation threatened him. I forgave him, but then became even more confused about who Christians are supposed to be.)

I went to work for the Bishop, but simply by association (being on his staff), I became the target of some clergy who felt that this bishop was not worthy to be a bishop. I saw church politics at its worst. Some of the clergy who had been my friends now became my enemies. Other clergy targeted me and refused to cooperate with any of the diocesan youth programs. They sat on the sidelines and were critical. They denied their youth any involvement in the diocesan youth programs. Intellectually or theologically, I could not even begin to understand that sort of thinking.

In the late 1960s, the Episcopal church introduced their newly revised ***Book of Common Prayer***. It had last been revised in 1928 and the world and language had changed considerably since then. A great deal of effort over many years went into the revision. The Prayer Book no longer used King James (16th century) words or concepts. I though it was a great new addition to the church in the 20th century. Many were confused. They liked the language of the 1928 BCP and knew much of it by rote. Some people were so adamantly opposed to the new BCP that they left the Episcopal church and started their own, called The Traditional Episcopal/ Anglican Church and kept the 1928 BCP intact. I had a difficult time believing this. The world had changed so much but some people had big problems changing with it. And what did the BCP have to do with the Good News? Next to nothing, as far as I could see.

Another hot button in the 1970s was the ordination of women. Women have been the backbone of Christianity from the beginning. The men followers ran off and hid when they crucified Jesus, but his women followers were there every step of the way. Look at any church. It's the women who do the lion's share of keeping the institution going. Our country was saying, if we really believe in "liberty and justice for all" we need to stop discrimination against women, people of color and those with different sexual orientations. But the church seemed to want to keep women in the background. Finally, some brave bishops took the bull by the horns and illegally ordained women. Again, another purging and groups left because they could not tolerate the idea of women having equal rights. For me, this was terribly confusing. I was starting to wonder, where was the church in which I had been ordained in 1960? It seemed to be disappearing.

Pope John the 23rd died in 1963, and it was not long after that the Roman Catholic Church seemed to start its long, slow return to pre-Vatican II times. John Paul II, very conservative, was elected Pope and for the quarter of a century of his leadership, he managed to take the church back to the 17th century. This was not only upsetting, but also very discouraging. The forward-moving church into which I had been ordained in 1960 was dying.

Then another negative reared its head. That had to do with missions, the heart of Christianity. As a child, I can remember that every Lent we were given "mite" boxes (little cardboard boxes with a money slot in the top which every one was supposed to fill with coins or bills) to support missionaries in their work overseas. I thought missionary work was the backbone of the church. I went into the mission field and after I was terminated from the youth church, I became the pastor to a small Hawaiian congregation in a low income, high crime community on O'ahu. It was a very fulfilling ministry. I then had a small mission church in the Marshall Islands and worked with the Marshallese on their islands in the South Pacific. Then in the 1970s, mainstream churches started to turn ecclesiastical control over to local churches, primarily in Third World countries. They did this very quickly, too quickly in my opinion. Most of the leadership in these areas was undereducated, naive about the rest of the world and unprepared to suddenly assume total control. Why did the church allow this to happen? So many mission churches have returned to 19th century theology and practices. Mainstream churches need to be much more involved in missionary work in the poor countries of the world. Ironically, the more evangelical (another word for fundamentalist) churches are very much involved in evangelizing in Third World countries and making tremendous strides. Why did the Episcopal church renege on its primary mission? It makes no sense.

When I went to seminary the open ordination of gays and lesbians was not even an issue. Supposedly, there weren't any in the church. Suddenly, as people with alternative lifestyles started demanding their "freedom and justice for all," the church discovered they had many clergy who were gay. Up to this point, they had been in the "closet." Now they were "out" and the church was terrified. They were forced to confront, in a very realistic way, Jesus' Great Commandment," to love self, neighbor (*including those with alternative lifestyles*) and Creation/Creator." Many churches were and still are not able to do this. They object when openly gay and lesbian individuals are ordained and consecrated. Now the church has a new splinter group, those who oppose giving full citizenship in the Kingdom to those who are not heterosexual. As a follower of a man who loved the literal and figurative "lepers" in his society, I am terribly confused. Why have so many of the so-called followers of Jesus not heard his call to love?

One of the more perplexing issues for me is what is happening in the Roman Catholic church concerning the sexual misbehavior of some of their clergy. It is not just a few. There are hundreds in this country alone. Think what the figures might be on a worldwide basis. It is like an epidemic. The fact that some clergy stray from their vow of celibacy isn't the confusing part. Clergy too are human. But my biggest confusion lies in the fact that the Roman Catholic church keeps trying to sweep the abuse issues under the carpet and pretend it does not happen. One has the feeling that they still are not dealing with the basic issue, compulsory celibacy for all clergy and nuns.

The Roman Catholic church's attempt to desexualize young people when they look at the church as a vocation is also mystifying. They take this wonderful creative gift of our sexuality and try to negate it at the height of young people's sexual prowess. Why? Celibacy certainly wasn't the tradition of the church passed on by Jesus. For seven centuries clergy could marry. Clergy marrying in all the other Christian denominations seems to work.

To make it even more difficult to understand, there are clergy in the Roman Catholic church who are married (legally) and have children. I had a Jesuit priest friend on Maui who fell in love with a wonderful woman. He left the Roman Catholic priesthood and married her. Then he was ordained an Episcopal priest. (This is not difficult to do because our theology/liturgy is very similar.) Some years later, he decided that he wanted to return to the Roman Catholic church. He applied to a Roman Catholic bishop and told him he and his family would be willing to pastor in a remote area where it was difficult to place clergy. He was accepted, reordained in the Roman church and sent off to a rural parish, with his family. I don't get it. Why can't all priests and nuns be married if they so desire?

More confusion. We hear over and over that marriage is sacred. Then why don't the Roman Catholics let their clergy marry? (Their idea of being "married to the church" is a cop out.) If it is so sacred, why does the Roman church issue annulments (if you fill out enough paperwork and perhaps make a substantial gift) to people who have been married for years? Instantly, this action makes the annulled couple either fornicators or adulterers and their children bastards! That one is a real baffler.

If marriage is so sacrosanct, why are some Christian churches a marriage factory? If one pays the fees, the church will often marry the couple with no preparation for marriage. As a result, in those churches on most Saturdays, there is one marriage after another and sometimes even during the week. That does not sound very sacred to me.

If a marriage does not work, why is the church so hard on divorcees? In some churches, divorced people are not even allowed to attend. A person either going through a divorce or having been divorced is shunned, excommunicated, and asked to leave the church. Divorcees are then denied the sacraments (are not allowed to receive "the Body and Blood"), cannot be remarried in the church and become second-class citizens. I thought the church was about love, acceptance and forgiveness, not judgment, rejection and damnation. This sort of thinking really befuddles me - especially in light of the ethics of Jesus.

Many people go back to the Old Testament for answers to ethical questions. I don't even begin to understand that approach. Parts of the Bible were written 4,000 years ago. The most recent portions of the New Testament were written shortly after the turn of the first century CE (Common Era). In the nineteen hundred years since the last writing was added to the Bible, the universe has changed radically. Values have changed. People have changed. We know so much more about life, the universe and living and we do it in a very different way than during the time of Moses, Jesus and Paul.

I guess if one looks hard enough in the Bible, one can find vague similarities between how people behaved 2,000 years ago and what is happening today. (People still have wars, try to destroy each other, steal, lie, etc.) However, in my eyes, it is two different worlds. I see people today (literalists) trying to fit the square peg (today's lifestyle) into the round hole (life 2,000 years ago.) It doesn't work. There are basic truths found throughout Scriptures. Jesus puts great emphasis on some of those ethical/moral principals. However, many of them need to be adapted to life today. It only confuses people when the church continues to live in a world that no longer exists.

That brings to mind the issue of the institutional church trying to run everyone's life, especially life in the bedroom. They do just as the Pharisees did in the time of Jesus. They love to have rules. When Jesus lived, Judaism had 613 laws they expected every Jew to follow if they were to have a relationship with their Creator. They had rules about everything imaginable. (To see a sampling, try to read the Book of Leviticus. It is very detailed and complex.) Today, the church has rules about what you can or can't eat, drink, do on Sundays, how to behave in the bedroom with whom and when, and who to have as friends or enemies. They will tell you how to vote, what stores to go to (look for the symbol of the "fish." It means that business is run by "real" Christians!), what music to listen to, the books you can not read, what to do with your fetus, prohibitions about dancing, how to spend your money, the minimum amount to give to them, what you have to do with free time and so forth. They are most invasive in a religion that was initially started to liberate believers from the law and give them back their freedom. Jesus wanted people to be responsible to and for themselves. Here is my befuddlement: Why doesn't the church simply give us guidelines for doing life and then let us work it out? The church does not seem to subscribe to Paul's statement, "work out your own salvation with fear and trembling." (Philippians 2:12b). Saint Augustine said it very clearly: "Love and do as you please."

How do Christians make ethical and moral decisions? Had you asked me this question fresh out of seminary, I would probably have given you either a very academic answer or I would have been stuck and given you some theological answer in "church-eze." Until I read Joe Fletcher's book, ***Situation Ethics***, I don't think I really knew how to make a practical Christian ethical/moral decision. I knew it had something to do with love, but it was not at all clear in my own mind.

I have a confession to share. I am a recovering homophobic, chauvinist, sexist, racist, bigot, anti-Semitic and murderer, just to name a few of the things I was before I discovered the ethics of Jesus. I was already an ordained priest before I started the recovery process.

Because my whole educational background has been in male only environments, I had this deep-seated feeling that this is a man's world. I was a closet sexist. One just had to look around and see who ran this planet. One did not find many women. The weaker sex was here to serve.

Because there were only a few black people in most of my surroundings, I had a deep-seated feeling that it was a white man's world. Of course, I gave lip service that this wasn't so, but deep down I felt blacks were "equal but separate."

Naturally, I would never admit that I was a bigot. Upon introspection, I then saw myself as a religious one. I had developed quiet prejudices against those who weren't Christians, Protestants and more especially the Anglican/ Episcopal brands. Jokingly, I would suggest that if Jesus came back he would certainly be an Episcopalian and would love ***The Book of Common Prayer***. After all, he wrote it.

Of course, it was the Jews who killed Jesus; just read the Gospel versions of his death and the events that led up to his crucifixion. Very subtly they will leave you with the impression that Jews were responsible.

I was an advocate for murder. If people did bad things, then it was our responsibility to make certain that those people were "fried" in the electric chair. "An eye for an eye" was necessary to keep bad folks in check. If they were murderers, then murder them. It is difficult to even remind myself that this was my thinking, some of it even after seminary. Then I discovered the ethics of Jesus (not the church's ethics) and my life changed. But I need to remind myself all the time that I am still recovering. Finding the ethics of Jesus also opened my eyes to a number of other issues. First, I must be very careful of what the institutional church tells me is truth concerning ethical issues. They can be wrong. The institutional church is BIG business. It has "franchises" everywhere and it seems to me very often the church is more interested in protecting the franchise than in building the Kingdom of Love. In my lifetime, the church has been wrong about remarrying people who have been divorced. Many of them were, and still are, dead wrong about not allowing women to be ordained. The church has consistently denied gays and lesbians full rights in the Kingdom. My point is this: The institutional church is not always the purveyor of *The Truth* Jesus presented.

I have learned not to blindly trust the Scriptures, especially the Old Testament. I have a difficult time with the god portrayed in much of the Old Testament. That god can be mean, vindictive, vengeful, unforgiving and unaccepting. That is ***NOT*** a god I would be the least interested in worshipping. I now take heed of what some of those in the New Testament state as ethical behavior. Paul was the architect of Christianity, but he was ***NOT*** the standard bearer for our ethical principles. Living in the 21st century, he is not helpful to me. As far as his ethics are concerned, in light of the ethics of Jesus, Paul was wrong most of the time. He was for slavery, against women, homophobic, had no idea what marriage was or is really about, and gave terrible advice about raising children. Let me emphasize this: my foundation stone, my standard, is Jesus. If Scripture does not hold up to his ethics, then it is wrong. He is my Christ, not the Bible. For me the so-called "Good Book" is the means, not the end.

Thirdly, simply because an ethical principal has been a long-time tradition of the institutional church does not make it correct. Compulsory celibacy in the Roman Catholic church has been around since the seventh century. Maybe it made some kind of sense then, but it certainly doesn't make any sense now. The Roman Catholics are having a difficult time recruiting clergy primarily because men want to be married. It's part of the orderliness of the Creation, and fun to boot.

One of the major problems in the church today is that Reason and Tradition prevail as the foundation of Christian ethics. Sometimes thoughtless excuses have become Reason and an oft repeated way of doing something becomes Tradition. Once established they become almost impossible to change. The institutional church needs a major overhaul, another reformation, but it appears that it would rather hang on to outdated traditions and misguided reasoning than return to the ethics of Jesus.

I believe that confusion abounds about what the guiding moral and ethical principles of the institutional church actually are or should be. I have a difficult time finding a Christian church that openly expresses the ethics of Jesus. As simple as his ethics are, the church seems to be constantly lost in the shuffle of intellectualism, academia, that institution's agenda, legalism or some other diversion. As a result, confusion rains…and everyone gets wet.

Amo ergo sum!
("I love, therefore I am!)

CHAPTER 2

THEOLOGICALLY SPEAKING…

Two men who lived in a small village got into a terrible dispute that they couldn't resolve so they decided to go to the town sage.

The first man went to the sage's home and told his version of what happened. When he finished, the sage said, "You're absolutely right!" The next night the second man went to the sage's home and told his side of the story. When he had finished the sage told him, "You're absolutely right!" Afterwards the sage's wife scolded her husband. "Those men told you two different stories and you told them both that they were absolutely right. That's impossible, they can't both be right"

The sage thought about it for a moment and then said to his wife, "You're absolutely right!"

I think my life would have been much easier had I developed the attitudc of the sage, everyone's right, at least as far as theology is concerned. But that is not me. My theology has changed radically from the day I walked into seminary, when they started to decimate my Sunday school foundation. In retrospect, the process was fascinating. It seemed that in the first year they tore down all the old thinking and then started to build the new. After three years in seminary, I thought I had my theology for life. Then I went into parish ministry, and my seminary theology was challenged with reality. It was the '60s and it seemed as if everything was being attacked: our values, our ways of life, our thinking. But I enjoyed that because I like being challenged, especially in the field of theology.

In this information age, things change even more quickly. Today's new is tomorrow's obsolete. So I think it is only fair that I now share with you where I am today in my theological thinking. I shall take certain Christian concepts, and share my thoughts.

GOD

My God is not in the image of a woman, or man. He/she does not live up there, wherever that might be. My God did not make the world in six days. She/he is not a "Master Puppeteer," "Benevolent Dictator," "The Terminator," "Santa Claus," a "Christian," "Vengeance," or "Dog Spelled Backwards," to mention a few misconceptions.

I believe that the word god is one of the more confounding words we have in our vocabulary. It means something different to each person, depending on that person's life experiences. There are some basic traits that most people's God has, but again, one can enter into a semantics exercise with the very words we do use.

I do not like many of the concepts about God found in the Old Testament. Sometimes when I read about the awful things that God is accused of doing, I want to have nothing to do with such a god. I realize that the Old Testament was written a long time ago, in a somewhat primitive society that had limited knowledge of the earth, and no understanding of the universe. But the world/universe has changed dramatically since the Old Testament was written. I now feel most uncomfortable when I hear Christians espousing many of these same antiquated concepts found in the Old Testament.

I prefer to use another terminology that does not have so much negative baggage. The general words I have chosen to use are Creator/Creation. Romans 1:25 influenced me with this concept as Paul states, "because they exchanged the truth about God for a lie and worshipped and served the creature rather than the ***Creator***." I am cognizant of the fact that these words still have anthropomorphic (human like) insinuations and are limited in scope. As far as I know there has been no human who can adequately describe God to everyone's satisfaction, and I shall not attempt to be the first. I like the "Anonymous" (Alcoholics Anonymous, Alanon, etc.) concept of a "Higher Power." In my opinion, it is a much more inclusive and non-threatening term.

The concept of evolution makes much more sense to me than creationism or its new friend, intelligent design. One of the ideas I like about evolution is that as the world and man evolve over thousands of years, so does the concept of God. To continue using an image of God that was developed over 4,000 years ago is not logical.

GOD IS LOVE

I suspect that you have heard the statement, "God is love." That works for me. But we also need to understand that God/Creator/Creation is much more than love. The Christian idea of God might be compared with our attempt to define the concept of universe. We have an idea of its vastness and understand some aspects of it, but our brain and limited knowledge prevent us from truly fathoming it all. Even with my educational background, I think I still have a limited understanding of God and can only use such simplistic phrases as "God is love!" to explain. As soon as I say that, however, I must now define the word "love." This is no simple task, but I am going to attempt to do that.

I like Bishop John Spong's definition of God: "I experience God as the source of love calling me to love wastefully all that God has made, including the earth with its plants and animals. I experience God, in the words of Paul Tillich, as the 'Ground of Being' calling me to be all I can be and to affirm the sacred being of all that is." (***Sins of Scripture***, Harper San Francisco, 2005, page 66)

WRATH OF GOD

The so-called wrath of God is often interpreted as the anger of the person "up there" who is running the show. It is like human anger, but has the ability to zap bad folks instantaneously. His wrath results in people with disabilities, 9/11, gang killings, cancer, heart attacks, hurricanes, murders and all the rest of the negative things that happen in our lives. The wrath concept is also the logic behind the idea that "it was their time" when a person dies, suddenly or otherwise. After all, the Master Puppeteer up there has a timetable for everyone and He/She is always on schedule.

Of course, I am being facetious, but almost on a daily basis I hear someone giving one of these excuses for why people die. The only reason I know that people die is because their brain/body stopped functioning. It could be a newborn baby or someone who has been around for decades. There is no such thing as a God "up there" who designs death. Death is simply a part of life.

People have disabilities because it is not a perfect world in which we live and unfortunate things can happen in utero, at birth, after birth, causing a disability. It is not something that is preordained and given to someone to make them stronger, or to punish them for theirs or their parent's sins.

For me, the wrath of God is simply the self-inflicted pain we do to ourselves when we refuse to love.

JESUS

He was a *total* human being who lived on earth about 2,000 years ago. Jesus was born of a human mother just like every other human being. He was probably raised in the farm land of Nazareth, lived in a large family (he had at least four brothers and two or more sisters. See Matthew 13:55-56, Mark 6:3)[1], probably learned carpentry skills or masonry from his ***father***, Joseph. We know nothing about him between the ages of 12 to about 28, and even though many stories are told about the boy Jesus I suspect they are pure myth. This is speculative, but some scholars have suggested that Jesus did not want to be a farmer or carpenter and went off to live with an ascetic group called Essenes, a very strict legalist group of predominantly Jewish folks who didn't believe in intercourse and guess what? They disappeared. At some point, Jesus realized this lifestyle was not for him.

He was born a Jew, died a Jew and was heavily involved in Judaism. He would have had no idea who/what a Christian is/was. There weren't any in his lifetime.

I do not ascribe to this theory most people think that he was not married. However, it is obvious he liked women and they liked him. He would not recognize himself as described in the New Testament, especially in the Gospel of John, in its entirety.

He was/is a great storyteller, preacher, teacher and a charismatic leader. Jesus was the right person, in the right place at the right time, with a message people were ready to hear. His words are still powerful today and, he still continues to revolutionize the world.

Some people suggest that he was/is the Son of God, but that only works if God is a human. I believe every human being is the son/daughter of Creator/Creation/Love. Jesus was divine, but so are you and I.

CHRIST

This is not Jesus' last name. He didn't have one. The word Christ is an adjective used to describe someone/some thing. Everyone has a Christ. It could be money, possessions, drugs, another person, cars, work, but always an object/person which one centers their life around. They feel that their christ is the center of their life. They focus a great deal of time, money, and effort into feeding their Christ. Jesus is my Christ because my life centers on what and how he tells me to do life. If he ever comes back here to earth, I would suggest that you not introduce him to your friends as Mr. Christ. It would be more appropriate to say, "This is my friend, Jesus bar Joseph" meaning Jesus the son of (in Hebrew "bar") Joseph. Who is your Christ?

VIRGIN BIRTH

The idea of virgin births worked in the Hellenized world in which Jesus was born. In Greek mythology, both men and women could produce babies just like that. But that mythology doesn't work today. It is a turn off for many people. It certainly was for Mark and John who never mentioned that myth in their Gospels, nor for Paul who never even suggested it.

Those stories (there are two very different fables in Matthew and Luke) developed after Jesus died. Today I consider both of them myths. The stories aren't literally true, but figuratively they are right on. The birth of Jesus from my perspective as a believer, tells me that although Jesus was created and born just like every other human being, his birth was special when one looks back at his impact on the world. So were the births of many of my other heroes.

RESURRECTION

I do not need a literal resurrection, but I do need a figurative one. I do believe that Jesus probably died by a crucifixion, engineered by and based on the jealousy, envy and hatred of Jesus by a few of his religion's religious leaders. (In this day and age I still see religious leaders figuratively "crucifying" people by their actions.) I have no idea if the tomb was really empty. Neither does anyone else, except as a faith response. The gospel of Mark in the original version does not tell an elaborate resurrection myth[2] nor does Paul (the earliest writer in the New Testament) stress resurrection in his early letters. I do not really care if the tomb was literally empty. I do care if the followers of Jesus really *felt his presence* after he was suddenly whisked away and murdered. They felt this presence so strongly that they revitalized his ministry and continued it in his name. From generation to generation believers have passed down this idea that Jesus is still with us. They feel his presence. His message of love is heard. His work of loving the world has continued for 2,000 years. I believe in the idea that love can "resurrect" people who, because of their past behavior, have died to themselves and others. For me, the heart of Christianity is not about a cross and empty tomb. It's about love that can transform/resurrect people's lives. The *real* Easter message is about hope, not a resurrected corpse. It is about turning our personal "good Fridays" (bad days/experiences) into Easters (moving on/new life in spite of the "good" Friday.)

HOLY SPIRIT

This is probably one of the more perplexing ideas in Christianity. When I was a child, the terminology was "Holy Ghost" which was a bit scary, and for me, vaguely associated with Halloween. They say that the Holy Spirit is part of the Trinity, another Christian concept that is equally as baffling.

I see the Holy Spirit as the spirit of love within each person. From the day we are born that spirit of love is there but it becomes suppressed. Babies are into the mode of survival and "me first." That trend keeps developing as that baby grows into adolescence and then adulthood. For some folks, "me first" never stops until they die. This is a problem for that person and those who surround him or her. People who are just into themselves are boring and difficult to be around for longer than five minutes.

One of the objectives of Christianity is to bring the spirit of love back to the surface. To also teach people how to not only love themselves, but more importantly how to love others as well as Creator/Creation. This does not happen easily.

Holy Spirit = Spirit of Love

THE BIBLE

It was written by men who were inspired by their concept of God and who shared their beliefs with words. I do not even begin to understand the idea that a god up there wrote it. Because I do not believe in an anthropomorphic (man-like) god, I can not envision Him, sitting up there, writing a book first in Hebrew, then Aramaic, next Greek and finally translating it into King James English.

The Bible has three parts. There is the Old Testament written by a wide variety of people who said some good things, but also said some things to which I could never subscribe. Some of the writers described their god as someone who is not nice and has no problem slaying folks who do not do what he wanted. As a Christian, for the most part, I concentrate on the **New Testament,** which portrays a God who is loving, accepting, forgiving and nice to have around.

The third book is the Apocrypha, a collection of stories not accepted by those who decided what ought and what ought not to be in the Old Testament. Many of these books are fascinating reading and much more interesting than some of the books we find in the Old Testament.

There is the same problem with the New Testament. Some of the books do nothing for me. I have no idea why the Book of Revelation or The Letter to the Hebrews were included. The former seems to be written as more of a science fiction piece and the latter being authored by a very boring person with a vivid imagination. I have finally stopped even trying to understand them or read them.

Most Christians are not at all familiar with the materials that were left out of the New Testament. They have missed the pleasure of reading such books as The Gospel of Thomas, The Gospel of Mary of Magdela (in which she tells of kissing Jesus on the lips), The Gospel of James, the Infancy Narratives of Jesus, The Secret Gospel of Mark and many more.

It is important to remember that a group of religious leaders (all men) in the fourth century chose what books were to be in all three sections of the Bible. Those involved were politically motivated, and as a result, there was a tremendous amount of name-calling, threats and intrigue involved in the process. Those who disagreed left that group and went off to start a new church. They also chose only what *they* wanted in the Bible. One might suggest that the Holy Spirit (the Spirit of Love) was not invited.

The Bible can be contradictory, confusing, fallible, boring and misinterpreted, but within its pages are great truths, which give us the way to do, or not to do life.

HEAVEN and HELL

Christians seem to spend a great deal of time wondering which of these places they will go to when they die. Most are certain that it will be to the latter, but very much want it to be the former. This always interests me, because neither place actually exists. They are the figment of someone's imagination. But they have made a great deal of money for the institutional church which, over the centuries, has designed elaborate methods for people to be able to buy or earn their way out of the "inferno."

For me, heaven and hell are real, but have to do with how we do life, or life does us. When things are going well, we feel like we are in a state of bliss or "heaven." When life is going poorly, we call it "hell." Most of the time we create our own heaven and hell both for ourselves and others.

SIN

Sin is one of the church's favorite words. Some clergy seem to enjoy telling people that they are in a constant state of sin. They have huge lists of all the sins that humanity can do and some of them even have lists of ways one can pay for having committed such sins. If your activity is fun, enjoyable and fattening it's probably a sin.

The word sin, for me, is like the word god. I don't use the word sin because it is overused and misunderstood. In lieu of sin, I prefer to use the word "separation." It is a condition that happens because of poor choices we make. We separate. Now there is a vacuum, a gulf, a barrier between us. Everyone does separation. But the Good News is that we can move through it easily if we are willing to accept responsibility, bury our pride and say, "I'm sorry!" Some people think Jesus didn't separate or sin, but if you read the Gospels carefully, you will see he separated from all sorts of folks. Ask the religious leaders, his family, the Romans, the woman from Samaria, the gentiles, the owner of the 3,000 pigs he drowned and on and on. For me, it does not seem as hostile or offensive to be in a state of separation as to be continually referred to as a sinner.

PERFECTION

There is no such thing as perfect or perfection - only in the eyes of the beholder. Jesus wasn't, you and I can't be, so don't bother trying. Many Christians think that by becoming perfect they have a ticket to that non-existent place called heaven. In the olden days the word perfect used to mean complete, which might make more sense in describing the actions of Jesus: He completed the will of God - to love.

PRAYER

This is probably one of the more interesting subjects in religion. There are many ways to pray and people have a tendency to think that it has to be very formal, using exact wording in order to have one's prayers "heard." It is not that difficult. There is informal prayer in which one allows their thoughts to lead. These thoughts can be anything one wishes. Some are directed inward concerning our own issues, others are to those whom we know are hurting. Many of our prayers are petitions requesting something, sometimes miracles. Too few of our prayers include praise, confession and thanksgivings.

Then there are formal prayers as found in prayer books, missals and liturgies. Some of these prayers have come to us from Judaism, the beginning of Christianity or centuries of usage. Many are beautifully worded and still relevant today. Some prayers use old misunderstood language that doesn't make much sense to many of us today.

Prayer works for many. It can be soothing, introspective and quieting. What it can't be is a shopping list telling God what it is that She or He needs to do for us and usually in a hurry. This approach doesn't work for me because my Creator has given me the freedom to do my life as I see fit, and the wisdom to work out the complications I bring into my life. Prayer centers me, defines the issue(s), and gives me the peace of mind and strength to meet the issue head on, and to start to resolve the problem(s). I do not expect divine intervention because there is no such thing.

For me, one of the great findings in the 20th century has been scientific proof that the power of prayer can heal people. There is something very healing knowing that many people, some known, many unknown, care for or love you. Love does heal.

THE TRINITY

I never have understood it and never will, because it doesn't make sense. There is no such doctrine in Scriptures except at the end of Matthew, where redactors decided to throw in the idea of Father, Son and Holy Spirit. (Matthew 28:19: "Go therefore and make disciples of all nations, baptizing them in the name of the Father and the Son and of the Holy Spirit,") This idea first appeared in about 180 CE. In 325 CE, the church fathers at the Council of Nicea and later at the Council of Constantinople (381 AD) decided to make it part of Christian dogma. For me, this was and still is a bad idea.

I find it sexist (it's an all male thing), limiting (everyone in it is sub-human), confusing (go ahead, explain it to me without using a bunch of theological double-talk), obsolete (many clergy refuse to even bring it up in a discussion because they can't explain it any better than I can) and unnecessary (the church functioned very well without it for a good many years).

SEX

This is one of our Creator's great gifts to humanity, but continually negated by the institutional church. I have no idea why the church wants to get into people's bedrooms and tell them what they can or can't do. I cannot fathom why a bunch of "neutered" old men in Rome have the audacity to tell people how to behave in their bedrooms. They have made this great gift sound dirty. I think that sexuality is a wonderful gift.

I think that each Christian's sexual activities are that person's business and responsibility. Paul says it very succinctly. "Work out your own salvation with fear and trembling." (Philippians 2:12)

CHURCH versus church

There is a vast difference between the above two words. The former is that group of believers who know that Jesus is their Christ. They worship him in a variety of ways but their lives are centered on love, acceptance and forgiveness. The latter is institutionalized religion or the "institutional church." They need money, property, laws, a hierarchy, lawyers and subscribers. They are political, self-indulged, always seem to be in controversy and are **BIG** business. Even though they often "poor talk" they have scads of money, property and investments. In spite of themselves, they are a necessary part of organized religion because they develop community, an important ingredient in our journey of faith. Unfortunately, organized religion is a turn off for many people who see it as a negative force in our culture. The church needs to work much harder to be The Church--those believers whose top priority is to love, just like Jesus taught them.

PREDESTINATION

This belief centers on the principle that someone "up there" has a plan for us, for every moment of our lives. This plan is instituted at the moment of birth and is the reason why anything or everything happens to us. It is why we trip on stairs, have auto accidents, are divorced, have gas, handicapped children and die. Predestination, even before we are born, knows when and how we shall live and die. It is unfathomable to me how many people believe this. So they now have permission to eat themselves into obesity, drive drunk, shoot their spouse or neighbor, abuse their child, be unemployed and be irresponsible. After all, "It's God's Plan!" The worst part is that there are many clergy who promote this revolting idea. It sounds so good! The only problem is officially, the church knows this is bad theology, and will have nothing to do with it.

The truth: There is no God Plan for everything we do on a daily basis. Each person is responsible for ***everything*** he or she does. If you do not believe this, ask the Presbyterians who at one point totally subscribed to the theology of predestination and then realized that life does not work that way.

There are many more words and/or phrases I could insert but we shall stop here. I simply wanted to give you an idea of my theological approach. It is different, but I am not a voice in the wilderness. My theology, after almost 50 years of reading, studying and discussing the Bible, the early church fathers and contemporary theologians, changes constantly. That is primarily because the world is changing rapidly. My adult life has been a learning and growing process that will continue until my dying days.

I call my thinking a systematic theology because it has developed in a systematic way starting with my concept of Creator/Creation. One piece develops on top of the other. My theology will never be finished because there is always something new coming forth. For instance, I am now working through all the newly surfaced old Gospels and documents that the early church fathers discarded as not worthy of being a part of the official Canonical Scriptures. These readings have given me new insights and a different perspective on my theology.

Some readers (if they have even read this far) will dislike (with different degrees of intensity) my approach and what I am saying. But I am asking them to stay with me, because I think the ethics of Jesus are the most important revelation in my life and can be in theirs. Some people will like what I am saying, perhaps with some minor disagreements, and are willing to expand their horizons further. Discussion and the sharing of ideas, wherever we are on the spectrum of agreement/disagreement, is an important part of our journey in faith.

Above all, I want to assure you that in no way do I think this book is God's answer to humanity, but it is food for thought as you develop your theology for daily living. I shall have accomplished my task if I can simply make you think further about your relationship with your Creator, God or Higher Power.

Let us now take a look at what I consider ***not*** to be the ethics of Jesus.

So whatever you wish that men would do to you, do so to them; for this is the law and the prophets." (Matthew 7:12) The Golden Rule

CHAPTER 3

WHAT JESUS' ETHICS AREN'T!

I found this on the Internet entitled, "Letters to God": "Dear God, Did you really mean, 'do unto others as they do unto you?' Because if you did, then I'm going to get my brother good!" One can only surmise that this child's brother was pounding away on him/her and if he/she did that, the siblings had the right to pound back. That child was trying to make the Golden Rule work for him/her because there was a real need to retaliate.

I use this as an example to demonstrate that people often take sayings from the Scripture and try to make them dovetail with their bias. This, I think, is the biggest problem we have in trying to understand the ethics of Jesus. There are so many other "ethics", systems or sayings found in Scripture, especially the Old Testament, that have little or nothing to do with what Jesus was telling us to do. But it is difficult to hear the message of Jesus when there are all these other misconceptions, which often have been drilled into our thinking for years.

Even though this might be construed as a negative approach, that is not my intention. What I would like to do is to briefly examine some of these "systems" to demonstrate, not that they are wrong, but they are ***not*** the ethics of Jesus.

What do you understand to be the ethics of Jesus? When I ask people the above question the response I hear most often is The Ten Commandments.

THE TEN COMMANDMENTS

Unfortunately, many Christians have been taught that the Ten Commandments are the basis of Christianity and its ethics. This can get people into trouble. This was exemplified in 2003 when the Chief Justice of the Supreme Court in Alabama was removed from his position because he insisted that a 5,280 pound slab of granite, on which were carved The Ten Commandments, stay in the rotunda of the court building. He thought that this carving, with its message, was appropriate for a government building in a country where we attempt (but often fail miserably) to keep a separation between church and state. Some people saw him as a hero, but others felt he was way off base. I think the Supreme Court Justice honestly believed that by displaying the Ten Commandments, he was promoting what he considered to be the foundation of our country, the Christian faith. Unfortunately, he lost his job and a part of his life because of this mistaken belief. I suspect that he still has no idea what the ethics of Jesus are.

Where did the commandments start? There are two variations in the Old Testament, Exodus 20:1-17 and Deuteronomy 5:6-21[1]. In Jewish history the commandments were given to Moses, by God, on Mount Sinai. The story tells about Moses going to the mountaintop to receive them. When he came back down his people were behaving rather badly, so in his disgust and anger, he smashed the tablets on the ground. Then he had to return to the mountaintop to do it all over again. Scholars suggest that this came about during the Jewish period of exile (ca. 587-530 BCE) and that these rules weren't necessarily original with the Jews. It seems that many advanced civilizations had a similar set of guidelines for their people.

The Ten Commandments are mentioned in the New Testament (Matthew 19:18; Mark 10:19; Luke 18:20)[2] primarily because Jesus, as a good Jew, had his faith built on the commandments and the law. However, as a practicing Jew he went back to early Jewish history, before the Ten

Commandments and cited Deuteronomy and Leviticus as the true foundation for living in the faith. He felt that the truth about how we are to live could be found in these two verses.

As child I had to memorize the Ten Commandments in Sunday school. It didn't make any difference that I had no concept of adultery, coveting, idols, murder or bearing false witness. I still had to memorize these rules if I wanted to receive my gold star. When we had Holy Communion back in the 1930s to 1960s, the Ten Commandments were read as part of the service, giving one the impression that they were very important to Christians. Early in my ministry I even preached a series of sermons on the commandments, unaware how outmoded they were. (A few years ago, I reread those sermons and, even in the privacy of my office, I was terribly embarrassed by what I had written as well as preached. I quickly put them in the circular file.)

Most Christians don't even come close to adhering to any of the commandments. Let's look at what the commandments state using Deuteronomy 5:1-22. The first commandment reads, "You shall have no other gods but me." First of all, I don't want to have much to do with the god portrayed so often in the Old Testament. That god is a "he" and referred to in very anthropomorphic terms. In other words, that god is very limited and can come across as a rather cranky old man who sat "up there," like a Master Puppeteer yanking strings, oftentimes making awful things happen to people. Ask Job. He was quick to smite either individuals or large groups of people. I envision "him" as someone I would not like to have as a neighbor. I certainly would not be interested in worshipping a god like that. I want to worship a god who is loving and accepting of all, forgiving and wonderful to have as a lifelong companion. Obviously, I cannot buy into that Old Testament portrayal of god.

The second commandment tells us, "You shall not make for yourself any graven image." Episcopalians fail that test badly. We have all kinds of crosses, sacred vessels, stone or wooden altars (which some priests kiss), vestments, the Book of Common Prayer, the Host (a piece of thin, dry wafer with images imprinted on them), the wine (referred to as the "blood of Jesus"), sacred buildings, just to mention a few of our graven images. The way I see many Christians worshipping the Bible (as if God "himself" wrote it) forces me to believe that often it too can be construed as a graven image. Do you truly obey the second commandment?

"You shall not take the name of the Lord your God in vain" is the third. If that were to mean saying a profanity almost everyone would be in trouble. However, what this commandment really refers to is the taking of oaths using God's name; i.e., in courtrooms, during the wedding ceremony, at baptisms/confirmations, ordination, in the military, when joining fraternities/sororities to name a few oath-taking ceremonies. I have taken many oaths with the name of God in them so again I miss the mark. How about you?

Next we are told to "observe the Sabbath." Remember the Sabbath is Saturday. I usually have a long list of Saturday jobs and the only thing I observe is that it's Saturday and time to do "honey do's." Now Sunday (not the Sabbath) is a bit different and will include some sort of religious observance. We, as Christians, celebrate the first day of the week (Sunday) as a reminder of that first Easter. A key word in this commandment is "observe." How that has changed over the years. As a child it meant going to church, having Sunday lunch (really dinner five hours early), doing something quiet around the house (like homework because there was no TV and all the stores were closed), early supper and off to church again. "Observe" today means something entirely different which could include church (unless one did it on Saturday) or playing a round of golf, or going to the shopping center or attending a sporting event, or having dinner sitting in front of the TV (probably falling asleep) and then off to bed. I fail again with this commandment. What do you do on the "Sabbath"?

The next commandment is one of the more interesting ones, "Honor your father and mother." It's a great concept. But as a psychotherapist I can assure you that this one could be dangerous - especially if your father is a drug addict (which means every sort of drug including cigarettes), a child molester, a womanizer, beats his children or is a macho-man. Or how about the mother who is into drugs, has affairs, is a prostitute, neglects her children or turns her back on the father who is physically abusive or molesting the children? Why would we ever suggest that we honor such a dysfunctional parent(s)? Sadly enough, it is this very commandment that has prevented many a child in an abusive situation from blowing the whistle. We only honor parents because of a behavior that deserves to be honored.

The sixth commandment suggests, "You shall not kill." Again a great idea, unless you believe in war (just or unjust), capital punishment, euthanasia, pro-choice, driving under the influence of some drug or committing suicide. Then obviously this commandment is not for you. Again, I don't pass muster. How are you doing?

Jesus made adherence to the seventh commandment very difficult. Deuteronomy states, "Neither shall you commit adultery." This is a good idea. However, Jesus added this caveat: One is not even to look at a woman lustfully or one commits adultery. (Matthew 5:27). I suspect there aren't too many men, or women, who are not guilty of that one.

Next we are told, "Neither shall you steal." Again, a very nice concept but, in reality, it might not work. Have you ever "borrowed" anything from the office? Kept too much change from a cashier? Forgotten to return a book from the library? During World War II the French Resistance stole as much as they could from the Germans. In Jesus' time there were the Zealots, freedom fighters of the first century, who stole from the Romans. Is the parent who steals food so their child won't starve to death wrong? Yes, but the greater good prevails here: One takes food in order to keep a child alive. Generally, this commandment works in a civilized society but one could list many exceptions to this legalist rigid rule.

We are faced with the last two commandments and up to this point I have not done well in obeying them. I could fail on the eighth also: "Neither shall you bear false witness against your neighbor." Now if taken literally it means that I shall tell the truth, probably in a courtroom, about the one neighbor we have. (There is no one living on the other side of us.) They are a very nice couple and I have a difficult time envisioning taking them to court. I would think we could resolve any issue we have outside of court. But suppose we did end up in court and we are each telling our side of the issue to the judge. I could say things that they might construe as false witness or visa versa. Sometimes truth as seen by one person is not truth in the eyes of the other person.

Some believe that this commandment really is about telling the truth, all the time. As a youth I remember seeing a play entitled, "Out of the Frying Pan." It was about a young man who had just graduated from college, had an excellent job and a lovely fiancée. He bet his roommate that he could tell the whole truth and nothing but the truth for a twenty-four hour period of time. The play takes the audience through the twenty-four hours with the young man *always* telling the truth. At the end of the twenty-four hours he had lost his job, his roommate and his fiancée, all because he told nothing but the truth. The point of the story is: Telling the truth is a noble idea but if one wants to live in the real world, one often must tell other than the truth. When you ask me, "How are you today?" you really don't want my list of medical ills nor all the things in my life that are not going well. If I want to keep you as a friend I shall lie to you and say "Fine!" even though that is not necessarily the truth. No matter how one interprets this commandment, I do not obey it.

The tenth commandment states, "Neither shall you covet your neighbor's wife...house...field...manservant... maid-servant... ox, (I can honestly say I have never been guilty of this one) ass...or anything that is your neighbor's." I would like to meet the person who has never coveted anything, or would I? Coveting is simply a part of being human. The major problem with coveting is not the coveting, but rather acting on that coveting. If one starts acting on it, then we are back to the eighth commandment… "Neither shall you steal."

The original Ten Commandments, by the time Jesus came, had become 613 commandments (laws). What Jesus saw was that the commandments -the laws - had taken over the lives of people, and that they were so busy keeping all the laws that they had no time for God or what it was that God really wants humanity to do…to love. In Matthew (5:17) Jesus tells us, "Think not that I have come to abolish the law and the prophets; I have come not to abolish them but to fulfill them." Later we are going to see how Jesus does this but for now I can assure you that his ethics were not built on the Ten Commandments.

THE GOLDEN RULE

Let us look at The Golden Rule. My favorite interpretation of this ancient saying is "He who has the gold, rules."

Jesus did use a saying we call the Golden Rule, but it was not until 1674 that it became known as the Golden Rule. A similar saying also is found in the Apocrypha in the Book of Tobit (4:15) and reads, "What you hate, do not do to anyone." Ideas similar to this are found in writings of the early Greeks, the Roman civilization, and can also be found in Hinduism, Buddhism, Islam and probably many other groups. I find The Golden Rule is a rather vague ideal rule of life. But, to many, it sounds good.

In Matthew (7:12) Jesus stated it this way: "So whatever you wish that men do to you, do so to them." Luke (6:31) puts it a bit differently: "And as you wish that men would do to you, do so to them." But this was not Jesus' ethic. As convincing as it sounds, I would strongly suggest that you not use this principal in raising your children. We do things to our children such as punishments, restrictions, time outs, being stern and assertive that we certainly don't want done to us as adults. Sometimes we have to resort to this behavior to get our children's attention.

I was an officer in the U.S. Marine Corps and never once in our leadership training did I ever hear the suggestion that The Golden Rule was the way to lead the troops. Nor, in boot camp, did I or any of my drill instructors, ever have the impression that this Rule was going to be the basis for our training as warriors.

I have met many a Christian who is proud to state that The Golden Rule is his/her foundation for doing life. Again, a nice concept but it is NOT the ethic of Jesus.

THE BEATITUDES

Some people would respond that they thought the ethics of Jesus were The Beatitudes. I felt they were just guessing and probably had no idea what Beatitudes really were. Sometimes they are referred to as "The Sermon on the Mount." The word beatitude is defined as "supreme blessedness; exalted happiness." (Random House, Webster's Unabridged Dictionary, Second Edition, 2001.) Some forms of beatitudes can be found in the Old Testament, the Apocryphal writings and in other parts of the New Testament. However, when people talk about The Beatitudes they are usually referring to a short section in the Gospel of Matthew (5:3-12) or even shorter in Luke (6:20-23)[3]. The scholars with the Jesus Seminar have suggested that perhaps verses 3, 4 and 6 of Matthew came from the mouth of Jesus, but the rest were not Jesus' thoughts. In Luke, they state that verses 20 and 21 are definitely sayings of Jesus. They also translate "blessed" as congratulations.

I have a problem when I envision myself walking into a low-income area, standing on a street corner or even a church and suggesting to the people, "Blessed are you, because you are poor." Worse yet, "Congratulations…you're poor." I have a feeling I might not come out alive. No one really wants to be poor, at least not anyone I have met. If I were to tell them "the poor will have a special place in the Kingdom," I think most of them would rather not have that special place. Some money would be much more useful.

I see The Beatitudes more of an eschatological (having to do with death and last things) rather than sociological issue or how we are to behave in today's world. In Matthew 5:21, "You shall not kill; and whoever kills shall be liable to judgment." That's tough; especially for those in the military, the police and some doctors just to mention a few. Perhaps what Jesus was suggesting was that there was too much killing going on and that in his Kingdom there would be no killings. This is very idealistic, but so are The Beatitudes. They do not necessarily help us in our everyday living.

There are some sayings after the initial Beatitudes that could be construed as Jesus' sayings concerning his ethic, but I see them as too arbitrary. In Matthew 5:22, Jesus is reputed to have said, "But I say to you anyone who is angry with his brother shall be liable to judgment; whoever insults his brother shall be liable to the council and whoever says, 'You fool!' shall be liable to the hell of fire." (I do not have a brother so does that mean I am off the hook?) The punishment does not seem to fit the crime. Who among us is going to make it? To me, the Kingdom or the ethics of Jesus is not about heavy judgment or exclusion. It is about the opposite - love and acceptance.

The Beatitudes also deal with those who mourn, the meek, the hungry, peacemakers and the persecuted in much the same eschatological fashion. Do this now and you will pick up "celestial brownie points" to cash in later, in heaven. Many of these sayings pertain much more to afterlife than how one is to behave today.

In this same section, Jesus discusses divorce[4] and comes down with a very heavy hand on those who do. In Mark[5] and Luke[6] Jesus also addresses divorce, but deals with it differently. Jesus, on the issue of divorce, sounds rather confused. As a result, for centuries the institutional church has been confused and has treated divorcees at about the same level as lepers or outcasts, at the bottom of the pile. That has changed a bit in my time, but I still see the institutional church handling divorce in a very legalistic, authoritarian fashion.

Supposedly Jesus spoke about retaliation[7]. He suggests, "If anyone strikes you on the right cheek, turn to him the other also." Please don't take this literally or there might not be much left of your cheeks. He then talks about "If anyone would sue you and take your coat, let him have your cloak as well; and if anyone forces you to go one mile go with him two miles." Jesus is really saying do not spend your life retaliating. It will eat you alive. Move on. We shall deal further with these kinds of issues when we discuss the ethics of Jesus, which are *not* the Beatitudes.

Before I started seminary in 1957 I did not know much about Paul. I had heard of him, but when lessons were read in church attributed to him, I usually could not understand what Paul was trying to say. He seemed complex, and when I heard or read his letters I felt stupid. (I still do, when a reader just jumps into reading one of his letters without any introduction or background information.) Then, in seminary, I was introduced to the total Paul, at least as much as we know about him, and I found him to be a very interesting person. In our Pauline classes we would spend hours reading his letters in Greek trying to decipher his intent. This process was complicated by the fact that there were no punctuation marks, no spaces between words, or indications of paragraphs, so we had to try figure out where all these ought to be. By the time I graduated, I thought Paul was a wonderful discovery. Some of his passages were elegant. He was the architect and draftsman of Christianity. He laid the foundation for Christian theology. I realized that he liked to boast a great deal and usually started his boasting with, "Even if I boast a little too much…" (2 Corinthians 10:8). He uses the word "boast" about 40 times in his writings. I learned that Paul was never married. (I think I know why not which I shall share that with you later.) He was controversial. It was usually his way, or the highway. He was very intelligent and had a systematic mind.

As I matured in the faith, I then began to question Paul about many of his ideas. Paul had a chauvinistic approach to women. He wanted women to be submissive to their husbands "Wives, be subject to your husbands...")[8] and probably to all males. Women in church should shave their heads[9] "For if a woman will not veil herself, then she should cut off her hair...") or cover her head and sit silently in the back of the church[10] (1 Corinthians 14:34: "women should be silent in the churches."). Children should blindly obey their parents[11]. "Children, obey your parents...even if your parents are sexually or emotionally abusing you." This was not good advice and has supported abusive parents for hundreds of years. He never spoke out against slavery. In an indirect way, because he accepted it as part of his culture, he condoned it.[12] "Slaves, obey your earthly masters with fear and trembling," For centuries Paul's permissive attitude toward slavery gave slave owners permission to enslave people.

Paul, in Romans 1:26[13], speaks out against homosexuals and lesbians. "Their women exchanged natural intercourse for unnatural, and the same way also men...") In 1 Corinthians[14] he states "male prostitutes" (there was no such word as "homosexual" in Greek) "will not inherit...the kingdom of God." These words of Paul have killed thousands or maybe even hundreds of thousands of men who might have a different sexual orientation than heterosexuals. His attitude about this and other value/morality issues can be diametrically opposed to the ethics of Jesus.

Christians (I was guilty of this one) have used these perverted ethics of Paul as a basis for their own value system. Today I find many people's homophobia so ingrained in their belief system that if Jesus came and told them that attitude was wrong they would crucify him *again.* What is interesting to me is that, over the years as I have learned about the gay lifestyle, I suspect Paul might have been homosexual. Perhaps this was his "a thorn was given to me in the flesh," as he stated in 2 Corinthians 12:7. In Paul's time, if it had been discovered that he was a homosexual, he stood an excellent chance of being stoned to death. If not that, then he would be treated as a leper in the Jewish and early Christian communities. Paul's sexual orientation really makes no difference to me. He is still a saint and a most worthy pioneer of Christianity.

I know Paul was very aware of the ethics of Jesus (I shall quote passages later), but he had a difficult time letting go of his Jewish, legalistic upbringing. I can identify with this. I spent six years being a Marine (1954-60) and once I had left the Corps to enter seminary I thought I had left all that behind. Even today, after I have dealt with an issue in an authoritarian fashion, my wife will remind me that my actions are much more that of a Marine than a loving caring Christian. The worst part is, she is right. I still manage to hang on to a little piece of my Marine life. Paul hung on to his Pharisaic background in spite of the fact that he knew better. But once we have read 1 Corinthians 13[15] we know that Paul understood very clearly the ethics of Jesus.

But Paul is *not* Jesus nor is he my Christ. I find that most of his efforts at being an ethicist miss the boat in today's world and I shall raise a red flag to those who would make the sayings of Paul 2,000 years ago the foundation for their Christian ethics today.

I shall now deal with a series of subjects that might be construed as the ethics of Jesus. I have no intention of going into them in depth but simply want to touch on them sharing some thoughts.

ANGLICAN ETHICS

In the fall of 2003, my wife and I went to Berkeley, California (the home of my seminary) to do some background research for this book. In many ways, that seminary experience was a disappointment. However, it was not so with the City of Berkeley, the Gold Country or the wine regions. All that was great. Primarily the disappointment was with the seminary, the Church Divinity School of the Pacific. I was saddened by the fact that there were very few young people going to seminary. The majority were middle-aged people with a few old people thrown into the mix. The Episcopal Church desperately needs young people who want to go into the ministry, if it wishes to remain relevant.

I audited a course entitled "Anglican Ethics," which I found to be in a typical Anglican style: intellectual, cumbersome and stuffy. I found it of little or no use to the person in the pews and probably not much help to those in the pulpit. There is no way I could ever preach about Anglican ethics. It is dull, boring and has little to do with the ethics of Jesus. As I sat in the classroom for four weeks, the major thought running through my head was, "No wonder the Episcopal church is dying!"

There is really no such thing as formalized Anglican ethics, but there is a methodology to which many Anglicans subscribe to make decisions. (I am not one of them). It is modeled after the teachings of Richard Hooker, an Anglican priest who flourished from about 1554 to 1600. He appealed to reason, scripture and tradition as the basis for making moral decisions. This is the same foundation used by many Anglicans today to make moral decisions. By reason, theologians mean nature or natural law, which is also the basis for moral theology in the Roman Catholic Church.

I have a problem with all three of these foundation stones in helping me make moral decisions. Nature or natural law is subject to a great deal of interpretation. That is why there are hundreds of books on the subject at the Graduate Theological Seminary Library in Berkeley. I have attempted to read a few of them but find them splitting hairs about rather unimportant things. They remind me of the Pharisees in Jesus' time who loved to split hairs and argue over trivia. (It was job security.) Most of the time, Jesus thought they were ridiculous[16]. I concur, especially in light of the ethics of Jesus.

One of my least favorite natural law teachings has to do with our sexuality. According to their adherents, there is only one purpose for sex, the procreation of children. Any other use of our sexuality is against the teachings of God. Proponents of natural law (mostly priests) use this primitive thinking to exclude anyone with an alternative lifestyle. Then they categorize anyone who uses sex for recreational purposes as sinful in the eyes of their god. This is not healthy thinking.

The next foundation stone for ethical decision-making is the Scriptures. You know my feelings about Scripture and its fallibility. There is no ethical decision I would ever make based on the life of King David, unless I want to use him as a negative model for adultery, murder, polygamy, reckless ambition and lousy fathering skills. I like David but he, along with a host of other folks in the Old and New Testament, had no day-to-day living experience that I would ever hold up to the ethics of Jesus. You know how I feel about Saint Paul. I admire him as the architect of Christian theology, but I disagree strongly with almost all of his ethical teachings. I use the ethical teachings found in so much of Scripture in a more negative way. It helps me determine what has *not* worked in the past and why the ethics of Jesus make so much sense.

Finally, we have tradition or some might call it past experience. Looking at the history of Christianity, I think many of these traditions are barnacles on the keel of progress. Because it has been a tradition to exclude homosexuals and lesbians from the Kingdom, it continues to be a tradition in spite of the fact that we understand a great deal more than did the Old Testament writers of 3,000 years ago. The real liberation of women began in the early 20th century, but there are still a large group of Christians who want to keep them submissive. The South seems to still be angry with the North because we took away their slaves. I guess that is why they fly their confederate flags. Recently, I have even heard a southerner suggest (with a straight face) that slaves were created by God, to make the life of the white man easier.

Then there is the church's antiquated thinking about people who have been divorced. There have been some improvements in my lifetime, but the church still treats divorcees as outcasts, especially if they would like to be remarried in the church. I could go on and on but I think the point has been made: Don't trust the traditions of the institutional church. For the most part, they seem to be self-serving.

I am discouraged with the present methodology of the Anglican ethics. They are practically useless to you and me, who must make moral decisions quickly and effectively. The ethics of Jesus will help us over this hurdle.

TRADITIONAL FAMILY VALUES

The phrase, Traditional Family Values, is thrown around a great deal by the fundamental/evangelical branches of Christianity. The people who espouse this value system claim that it is based on Scripture and insinuate that this is the way Jesus wants us to live. I can't deny that the concept of Traditional Family Values is based on Scriptures, some of which were written as long as 4,000 years ago and have not had new input in 1,900 years. But the world is a very different place than it was in the time of King David, Jesus or Paul. Essentially, they were addressing issues in their world, which they thought was flat, centered around the Earth and had a heaven up there. Compared to us today, they had limited knowledge and saw life much differently. Men reigned supreme and for the most part women were treated as property. Children were practically slaves. There was a huge divide between the rich and the poor. Medical knowledge was almost non-existent. God was referred to only in the male gender and "He" appeared to be primarily a smiter of those who did not do what they were supposed to do. Men with their own agenda established the rules of how one was to behave in their society.

The proponents of Traditional Family Values are still primarily men (many are out-and-out chauvinists) who love to keep women submissive and children like little robots.

They justify their bigotry with their interpretation of Scripture.

Whenever I hear about Traditional Family Values my first question is, “Whose tradition?” I hope not Jesus’ family. As far as I can see, it was a rather dysfunctional family. He did have a mother, Mary, and a father, Joseph. Speculation suggests that Joseph was much older than Mary (perhaps she was 13 to 16 years old when she was married) and that he was not around for more than 15 to 20 years after Jesus was born. Jesus had brothers and sisters. Matthew (13:55-56) names the brothers, “James and Joseph and Simon and Judas” and then states, “Are not all his *sisters* with us?” Mark (6:3) leaves out Joseph and substitutes him with Joses. (Where did that come from?) We do not hear much about them, except for James who is reputed to have become a follower. After the death of Jesus, he became a leader in the church in Jerusalem. At one point, early in Jesus’ ministry, when he returned to Nazareth and preached in the synagogue, his family thought he was strange (perhaps he had a demon) and wanted to stone him to death[17]. There were rifts within the family. Jesus felt like an outsider and unwelcome. Are these the family values to which we are to adhere? I hope not.

Or am I to subscribe to the family values of my childhood family? My father was the head of the household. My mother did not work outside the home. (Even though she was a teacher, as the wife of a clergyman, she was forbidden to work outside the home.) Outwardly she was submissive to my father. After high school I went to college. My sisters did not. Sundays were “blue.” No stores or bars were open. There were no such things as a television or a computer or a cell phone. We had only one car. The blacks lived up the street, but were relegated to being maids, servants and trash collectors. There were no homosexuals or lesbians, or so one thought. I could continue, but I suspect you see the point. The only Traditional Family Values there are in our society, are the ones set up by our immediate families. In our culture, the next generation will have another set of values.

Let's face it. Traditional Family Values is a phrase established by people who want to keep men running the world and women and children a lesser breed. Does it have anything to do with the ethics of Jesus? Absolutely nothing, so let's cross it off the list.

I suspect you have had enough of what Jesus' ethics aren't. I have too, so I shall conclude this chapter with the idea that Christian ethics are not the ethics of Jesus. I use my own church as an example of what they are not. I could probably go through every major Christian denomination and demonstrate the same thing. Each Christian denomination became a denomination because they broke away from another denomination. With the split came some of the old ethics of that denomination, and some different ethics with a heavy emphasis on what the new group felt was important. One must also remember that for the most part it was/is a select few (predominantly men) who established the system and who keep it in line. Most clergy/pastors/priests do not have the time or the inclination to spend the hours of research, meetings and study that it takes to understand or develop a system of moral or theological ethics. So students in seminary are presented with what the ethics of that denomination are, and then at ordination vow that they will adhere to that system. In my seminary, there was little time for discussing, questioning and evaluating our ethical/moral theology. It was after 20 years of seeing my denomination's ethics in action that I began to question whether it had anything to do with the ethics of Jesus. At this stage, I would suggest that there are not many folks, clergy or laity, who can easily state the ethics of Jesus.

It is time to look at what his ethics are.

"You shall love the Lord your God…and your neighbor as yourself. There is no other commandment greater than these." (Mark 12:30-31)

CHAPTER 4

THE ETHICS OF JESUS

Sign on a bumper sticker: "Love your enemies. It really gets them confused!"

I have a very old "Non Sequitur" comic entitled, "Moses and the First Draft" Moses is standing in front of a stone plaque that reads "DON'T DO BAD THINGS" and is saying to the group gathered around, "It might leave a little too much room for rationalization. Maybe you should try to break it down to a few specifics."

Jesus did just that and it is called the Summary of the Law or the Great Commandment. However, before we go into the sayings, allow me to share a few reminders:

1. Jesus is my Christ. My Christ is not: the Bible (especially the Old Testament); the institutional church; the Golden Rule; Saint Paul or any of the things I mentioned in the previous chapter. As my hero, guiding light, whatever name I give him, it is the things Jesus is reputed to have stated in the four gospels where I find his ethics. However, I have looked in all the letters of the New Testament to see if the main message of Jesus was heard and passed on to a new generation. (It was and I shall give details later.)
2. Jesus was born a Jew, lived his whole life as a practicing Jew and died a Jew. His Scriptures

were the books of the Old Testament and it appears he knew them well. If he were to come back today and someone told him that he was the founder of a religion called Christianity, his followers are called Christians and that he is proclaimed as the Christ, Jesus would probably have no idea what you were trying to tell him.

3. As a practicing Jew, Jesus lived under the 613 laws prescribed by his faith as the way to have a relationship with Yahweh. He obviously saw a problem with his fellow Jews living under the Law. They were so engrossed in following the laws that they ignored issues such as justice, mercy and love. Jesus then went back to early Jewish history. He suggested that one statement made in the Book of Leviticus and one in Deuteronomy, were the standards by which Jews needed to live. The 613 laws had outlived their usefulness. This pronouncement by an ordinary peasant upset some of the religious leadership of Judaism, and he became a marked man. As we all know, eventually a few of the religious leaders "quieted" Jesus. (Crucifixion has a way of doing that). One might say a few of the Jewish priests, lawyers and scribes won the battle (they were rid of a pesky, rabble rousing nuisance), but lost the war. A powerful new religion was founded.

4. I don't know if in his time Jesus was seen as a radical revolutionary (he was so quiet about it). But looking back some 2,000 years, there is no question that he revolutionized his world and is still revolutionizing our world with his radical thinking. The world has not been the same since Jesus started preaching.

5. Jesus realized that adhering to the Law was not the solution to having a relationship with Yahweh. Fact is, he saw the Law as the major problem within Judaism and suggested some

changes. The problem with adhering to the Law is that it becomes the most important thing, and the reason for the Law (to love Yahweh) becomes lost in the shuffle. Jesus could see that "loving" the Law, crossing every "t" and dotting every "i," had become much more important in Judaism in his time than "loving" people, all people, in every sort and condition.

Jesus then went back hundreds of years in Jewish history to the Pentateuch (the Five Books of Moses, or the first five books of the Old Testament) and from the Book of Deuteronomy 6:5 pulls the phrase, "You shall love the Lord your God with all your heart, and with all your soul and with all your might." Then, he goes to the Book of Leviticus 19:18b and pulls the phrase, "You shall love your neighbor as yourself." In the New Testament, these become The Great Commandment or as some call it, "The Summary of the Law".

In the Gospels of Matthew, Mark and Luke[1], it all starts with the same setting. Jesus is surrounded by some religious leaders. Matthew calls them Pharisees, Mark calls them "scribes" (scholars and teachers of Jewish law) while Luke has one person, "a lawyer". They then ask Jesus a question. Matthew has one of the Pharisees, a lawyer, ask Jesus, "Teacher, which is the greatest commandment in the law?" Mark has one of the scribes ask, "Which commandment is first of all?" Luke's lawyer demands, "Teacher, what shall I do to inherit eternal life?" Except for some word order changes, Jesus tells them about the same thing. Luke puts it this way: "You shall love the Lord your God with all your heart, and with all your soul, and with all your strength, and with all your mind; and your neighbor as yourself." Matthew concludes the section by stating, "On these two commandments depend all the law and the prophets." In other words, it is the Great Commandment that sums up all the laws in the Old Testament. In Mark, Jesus says, "There is no other commandment greater than these." In Luke, he concludes with, "...do this, and you will live."

The Gospel of John relates the story in a different way. It is toward the end of Jesus' life and he is giving his disciples instructions. In John 13:34, Jesus states, "A new commandment I give to you, that you love one another; even as I have loved you that you also love one another. By this all men will know that you are my disciples, if you have love for one another."

Can it be any clearer as to what the ethics of Jesus are? They are all about love. Jesus even goes so far as to suggest that we are to love our enemies[2]. Wow! That's a toughie! Jesus is telling us the Law is out and love is in? Can it be any clearer what it is that we as followers are to do? We are to be lovers of ourselves, our fellow human beings and of Creation and our Creator.

With this in mind let me go to the next step. As I have suggested previously, in no way can I describe God. I believe the concept of God is beyond human comprehension. For thousands of years man has tried to describe God in human terms, but in the age of information/technology this doesn't cut it for many. The universe is too vast to put a human spin on God. In my own limited way, I have tried to remove the human concept of God from my vocabulary and have used the term(s) Creator/Creation. There is another way I would like to describe this phenomenon we call God, but it always sounds too simplistic and might be construed as trite. But let me share it with you anyway. I would like to say that God is love and love is God!

One of the treasured books on my shelves is Gregg Easterbrook's ***Beside Still Waters, Searching for Meaning in an Age of Doubt,*** (William Morrow and Company, Inc., 1998, New York.) Let me share some of these thoughts. "Such was his gift that Jesus simplified the entire structure of spirituality into a single unitary sentence. 'This is my commandment, that you love one another as I have loved you.' … The Commandments have fallen from Ten…to One, and encountering the One Commandment, we find the focus entirely on the human." (page 313). Three pages later, Gregg shares "a few spiritual truths anyone might accept…First, heaven asks nothing for itself…the divine yearns solely for human tenderness and virtue. Second, God had to grow spiritually: from belligerence to nonviolence, from vehement fame to still waters...Third, spiritual compassion holds the potential for resolving the world's ills...Fourth, life has meaning...Fifth, everything ineffable (inexpressible) can be conveyed in a three-word phrase found in some form in the writings of every faith: '*God is love*.' The author of First John wrote, 'So we have known and believe the love that God has for us. God is love, and those who abide in love abide in God, and God abides in them...' This verse is astonishing both in its buoyant expectation for the human prospect and in its simple factual declaration." (pages 316 and 317) AMEN!

So if we subscribe to the idea that God is love (a partial definition) and believe that Jesus is our Christ, then I think the ethics of Jesus have to be based on love. Whatever the issue, love is the answer. Clearly, this is an over simplification that needs clarification.

Even though "love" is only a four-letter word, it is a very complex concept. In the English language, it is especially difficult, because we have only one word that expresses a huge variety of degrees of love. Fortunately, the Greek language, in which the New Testament was written, does use different words. In the next chapter, I shall be defining and discussing these ideas of love.

I leave you with these words written over 1,900 years ago, but which are still germane today. The Pharisees are confronting Jesus and ask, "Why do your disciples not live according to the tradition of the elders, but eat with hands defiled?"[3] There was a law in Judaism that everyone must wash their hands before eating. If only for health reasons, this is a good idea, but sometimes not always possible--especially back in those days without running water. Jesus then attacks and calls them "hypocrites," quotes Isaiah (29:13): "This people honors me with their lips but their heart is far from me; in vain do they worship me, teaching as doctrines the precepts of men." Then Jesus hits them with one of his zingers: "You have a fine way of rejecting the commandment of God (love) and hold fast the tradition of men."[3]

Some 1,900 years later I feel that institutional Christianity is in much the same place as were the Pharisees back then. There are too many laws, rules, regulations and rubrics. I would like very much to be an instrument of change, to try to bring the church back to where it needs to be, so that it can be effective in today's world. If that is to be, we need to make certain that its foundation is about love, not law.

"My little ones, let's not talk about love.
Let's put love into action and make it real."
***Cotton Patch Version of the Bible,* I John 3:18**

CHAPTER 5

LET'S DEFINE TERMS

A man was walking along a California beach and was deep in prayer. All of a sudden, he said out loud, "Lord, please grant me one wish?" Suddenly the sky opened and in a booming voice, the Lord said, "You have been a faithful servant to me in all ways so I shall grant you one wish."

The man responded, "Please build me a bridge to Hawai'i so that I can drive there any time I want." There was a long silence and then the Lord replied, "My son, that is a very materialistic wish. Think of the enormous challenges it would take just to build that bridge. The supports would have to reach the bottom of the Pacific. Think of all the steel and concrete it would take. That wish is just too materialistic for me. Please think of another wish."

The man thought for a few minutes and then asked, "Lord, I wish that I could understand women. I want to know what they think inside their heads, why they give me the silent treatment, why they cry so much, what they mean when they say, 'Nothing!' and how I can make a woman truly happy."

There was a long pause and then the booming voice came back, "Do you want that to be a two or four lane bridge?"

Our primary task in this chapter is to define many of the terms that I shall be using in the rest of the book. It is important that you, the reader, understand what it is that I mean (not what others mean) when I use a certain term or phrase. I am going to start with the word "love," which has many of the same challenges as trying to "understand women." (That's another book!). In the English language there is only one word to signify that something is very important to that person. People talk about loving their significant other, their pet, their car, ice cream, wine, a movie and on and on, but use the same word. There is a great deal of difference in the intensity of a love one feels for their significant other, than for their favorite movie.

Unfortunately, no one but the speaker really understands the intensity. I have known people who talk about how much they love their husband or wife and how much they love their pet. What is the difference between those loves? I have had people in therapy who have told me that they love their spouse, but their pet gave them what they wanted, unconditional love. Their spouse gave them a love with all kinds of conditions.

The major language of the early New Testament writings was Greek. There are a few manuscripts in Aramaic. Jesus probably was not a fluent Greek speaker, but since it was the major language of the Romans, he would understand and maybe even speak some. His everyday language was Aramaic, a Semitic dialect related to Hebrew. Being a practicing Jew, he also spoke Hebrew. But it is to the Greek language we shall look for our study of the word "love."

The Greeks had four different words for love, each signifying a different meaning and intensity. The lowest in intensity is *philia*, a love that exists between friends, people at work and maybe even things. There are cities called Philadelphia in our country and this translates into "the city of brotherly love." Realistically speaking, *philia* is probably closer to "like" than love. It demands something in return such as acknowledgement, a certain level of caring and usually a minimum kind of involvement. If that something does not happen to the satisfaction of the giver or receiver, then the relationship is broken. There is not much of an emotional involvement, so with perhaps little or no pain, people move on with their lives.

The next level of love is called *storge*. It is the affection between siblings or with one's parents or relatives. Maybe we don't even like the person, but if anyone says or does anything negative, we rise to their defense. Our middle daughter is multi-handicapped, and as a child she had to take a bus to school. When she was in about the seventh or eighth grade there was a boy on the bus, also challenged, who used to pick on our daughter. Her older sister found out about it and the next afternoon when our daughter came home on the bus, our oldest daughter (by two years) got on the bus and, in sign language, told the young man who was picking on our daughter that if he ever picked on her sister again, he would regret it, maybe for the rest of his life. He never picked on her again and sat as far away from her on the bus as he could. The interesting point to my wife and me was that at home the two sisters seemed to have plenty of sibling conflict, but someone outside of our family could not treat her sister badly. This is *storge* love, which does demand something in return. Again, if it isn't forthcoming the relationship is usually finished.

Our next love word is *eros* or erotic love involving our sexual/sensual being. This love exists between husbands and wives or between two people committed to each other. It is a much deeper love than the above two. It ties into our emotions and very definitely demands something in return. Without a reciprocal involvement, eros is not going to go very far.

The fourth kind of love is very different. The Greeks call it *agape*. It demands nothing in return and needs to be given freely with no strings attached. It cannot be earned, purchased, pleaded for or cajoled. *Agape* is the word Jesus most often uses in the Gospels and is the primary word for love found in the Greek versions of the New Testament. This kind of love is more difficult to achieve, because, as fallible human beings, we almost always expect something in return either directly or indirectly. Allow me to share an incident in my life, which, in retrospect, could be classified as *agape*.

In the summers during my college years, I was a lifeguard on the beaches of Stone Harbor, New Jersey. Stone Harbor is situated on a seven-mile long island, on the Atlantic coastline. The island consisted of two towns, Stone Harbor to the south and Avalon in the north. The latter was then underdeveloped, and had a large section where the beaches were empty and unguarded. On this particular day, I was seated on the last lifeguard stand on 82nd Street, the last guarded beach of Stone Harbor. The surf on that day was rough and the waves big. I was alone on the stand and noticed a boy frantically riding his bicycle up the beach from Avalon. When he arrived at my stand, very much out of breath, he yelled, "A little girl is drowning on 67th Street. Can you help?" I could have said, "Sorry, my friend, but that's Avalon and we are not paid to guard that beach," and that would have been the end of that. Instead I said to the boy, "Lend me your bike. I'll blow my whistle and other guards will come to my stand. You tell them what's happening. They'll drive you to your bike."

I took off on his three quarter size bike in the sand, 15 blocks of it. Fortunately, as lifeguards we had to stay in top shape. Still it was a tough ride. In the distance, I could see a small group of people gathered on the beach waving and shouting. I rode up. "Where is the little girl?" No one spoke English. They pointed to the sea and I just caught a glimpse of the girl quite a way out to sea. They told me in very broken English, "She no swim!" With hand signs I told them I would start toward her, but I couldn't see the girl, so when they saw me raise my hand they needed to point toward the direction I should swim. They seemed to understand. I ran into the surf and moved quickly through the crashing waves. I started in the direction where I thought the girl should be. Every once in awhile, I could see her head bobbing on the crest of a wave. A few times I had to signal to shore for hand signals, to point me in the right direction. Soon I was close enough to keep a very steady eye on her. It was a miracle that she was still above the water, because she had been bobbing around for at least half an hour. Finally I reached her. She was about 12 years old, scared and exhausted. When I arrived she almost jumped out of the water on me, and then proceeded to throw up, on me. I put a crosscheck carry on her and started toward the shore. By this time quite a crowd had gathered on the beach, emergency vehicles had arrived and other lifeguards were in the water with buoys heading toward me. We put her on the buoy and the guards on shore pulled us in quickly.

Immediately, medical personnel began resuscitation. I was sitting on the beach when the Captain of the Stone Harbor lifeguards came over and asked me how I was? "Fine!" I replied. Then they put the little girl in the ambulance and took her to the hospital. I jumped in the lifeguard jeep and was driven back to my duty station. I climbed on my stand and resumed my duty as if nothing had happened. There was no further mention of it. We did find out the next day that the little girl would be fine, but needed to stay in the hospital a few more days for observation.

Why is this *agape*? It was unconditional love asking nothing in return. It was given freely. It included risk, maybe even my life. I never expected a thank you or any sort of recognition. I was just doing what I had to do, risking my life to save the life of another, a person I did not even know.

Someone once suggested to me that as soon as I told the story it was no longer *agape,* because having told the story there was now something in it for me. People would think I was wonderful and I might become a hero in their eyes. Now it became a bragger's story. Oh well, at least while it was going on, it was *agape*. It is this *agape* love to which followers of Jesus subscribe.

There are some other traits about *agape* that are important to remember. This love accepts everyone for who they are. It does not start with what one wants the other person to be. If one is gay or lesbian, that is who they are and one must accept him/her/them. Too many religious institutions want to take away people's sexual orientation and change them to their side. That is not *agape*. That is love, with conditions.

Drug addicts/alcoholics must be accepted for who they are. This is why the many Anonymous Programs have been successful with so many people. There is no judgment. But that does not mean there is no tough love. There is plenty of that, but the final decision of what the addict is going to do with their life is up to the addict. To me, this is so much more loving than the judgment of many religious people. One time in my multi-faceted career, I was the Director of a drug treatment program in California. My senior counselor was a man who had spent a great deal of his adult life on skid row. He really understood what it was like to be down and out. He loved to tell me and the patients how he had accepted Jesus as his Christ, 117 times. Every time he needed a meal or shelter or something from a skid row rescue mission, he would accept Jesus, get what he wanted, and then forget about Jesus. I think Jesus would want us to love the person where they are and then give that individual what he/she needed. If someone should inquire (highly unlikely with addicts), then explain the motivation behind the love.

Jesus has suggested that, "For you always have the poor with you," (Matthew 26:11). I do not believe that anyone really wants to be poor, but for all kinds of reasons people are poor. Some start (and finish) that way in life, and to others it happens along the way. *Agape* is not concerned with how people became poor. *Agape* simply responds. Unfortunately, too many people in the church and in our country blame the poor for being that way and do not really want to help. Over and over I have heard, "It's their fault. They need to pull themselves up by their bootstraps and get to work. And furthermore, don't bring your dirty smelly body into our church."

Forgiveness is another feature of *agape*. It must be given freely and quickly, no matter what the circumstances. This does *not* mean forgive and forget. That is one of those trite phrases that does not make any sense. When something happens to or against us, we are going to remember that incident, perhaps for the rest of our lives. For me, the much better saying is, "Forgive and move on with your life." Many people cannot do this. They center their lives on this awful thing and allow it to absorb every bit of creativity they might have. Not being forgiving of oneself or of others destroys lives. Forgiveness is a must, both for the sake of the giver and the receiver. How many times do we forgive a person? Three or four? Jesus suggests "seventy times seven" (Matthew 18:22) which translates into an infinite number. That is tough, but it is *agape*.

Let me share a story about forgiveness and its power. Dr. Richard Grayson was a psychologist in southern California. In 1987 a man and a woman forced their way into his home, killed his wife and robbed the house. The woman was young, just 16 years old. She had fallen under the influence of her older companion. Both were drug addicts. They were caught and brought to trial. Grayson wanted revenge and considered buying a gun, walking into the courtroom and blowing them away. His life was completely consumed by anger and revenge, so much so that he became physically sick. He then came to the conclusion that he had to forgive his wife's killers, and he did. One of his sons, 13 years old when his mother was murdered and at 29, seemed to still be very angry, thought his father was crazy and asked, "Does he think he's Jesus?" (That's an interesting comment.) Watching his son's anger, Dr. Grayson's life changed. Not only has he forgiven both of his wife's killers, but he is also working on a plan to have the woman who was involved in the killing, released from prison. It seems that, at the time of the crime, the woman was very young and on drugs. In prison, she had turned her life around. She was a model prisoner, had devoted herself to her art, was tutoring other prisoners and helping women who were HIV positive. Dr. Grayson was impressed and felt that someone who shows that much initiative in turning her life around, ought to be given another chance on the outside. This is the power of forgiveness: It changes lives and allows people to live in freedom.

We are now going to change gears a bit and define other terms such as values, morals, morality and ethics. Let us start with the word ethics. I am sure you are aware that this book is not called *The Ethics of Christianity* because I believe there is a vast difference between the ethics of Jesus and those of the institutional church. As I have shared with you, I became acutely aware of this when I spent a month at my seminary and monitored a course entitled "Anglican Ethics." The professor and the students hardly ever, if at all, discussed the ethics of Jesus. When I use the term ethics I mean, how a follower of Jesus ought to behave toward oneself, toward every other human and toward our Creator/Creation. The ***"Dictionary of Ethics***" defines ethics as "rules of conduct recognized in respect to a particular of human actions" (page 665). Rather simple, isn't it?

For me, the word moral(s) means the principals of right conduct based on the ethics of Jesus. These principals can be diametrically opposed to the rules of society or even the institutional church. This could make practicing the ethics of Jesus difficult, because it often seems that the ethics of Jesus are saying one thing and the church another. For instance, Jesus tells us to forgive others an infinite number of times, 70 times 7. As far as a divorcee being remarried in the church, the institution either will not forgive (no remarriage) or at the most only allow a divorcee to remarry two times. There does not seem to be a great deal of forgiveness there. To me, this is most inconsistent.

When I use the word value(s), I mean the quality(s) desirable as the means or an end in itself. If our end is love, then our values must include such qualities as unconditional acceptance and forgiveness. In my opinion, values and morals are very closely aligned and mean almost the same thing.

When I use the concept of morality, I am using a word that is often used in a secular society. Here in the United States, we have a sense of morality. It differs from other countries. In the US, for the most part, to show naked breasts can be offensive. In many countries of Africa and other parts of the world, women walk around with no covering over their breasts and no one seems to care, except missionaries.

We go to France every summer or fall, and on the beaches there are women without any bathing suit tops. In some of their ads, women show bare breasts and the "morality" police (or other police) are not on their cases yelling "Shame! Shame!" In the US, a woman who bares her breasts could be arrested for indecent exposure. Our morality code says exposed breasts are out of bounds. In France, their morality accepts bare breasts. For me, morality and the ethics of Jesus are different things. The morality of our society is not dependent on religion. For me, the ethics of Jesus are not dependent upon, nor do they necessarily have anything to do with, the morality of our society. My morality is based on the ethics of Jesus and not on the laws of the USA.

An example: abortion in our country is a big issue that doesn't seem to go away. The issue is constantly kept in the forefront primarily because of institutional religion. Some groups want it their way, pro-life. On the other end of the issue are those who believe in pro-choice. It is impossible to be in the middle of this issue, unless one doesn't care. Those who don't care are not really involved in the ongoing debate. I happen to be pro-choice. (Surprised?) Why? It starts with my ethics in which I believe that every human being is responsible for himself or herself. The only person for whom I am responsible is Bil Aulenbach. My wife and I had a responsibility for our children as they were growing up, but when they became 18 we turned that responsibility over to them. If a woman wants an abortion, I want her to make a responsible decision, based on unbiased information that she seeks. If she chooses abortion, then I want her to have a medically based one, not one with a coat hanger in a dingy, dirty hotel room. Does that mean I am pro-abortion? Not at all! I would hope for that "perfect" society in which abortion would not even be a reality. But we don't live in such a world, and people do make bad choices. My ethics tell me that I must even love/support people who make poor choices. I am not their judge, nor am I responsible for them. They will pay a price for that abortion (unless they are sociopaths) for the rest of their lives. My role is simply to be there to love and accept them through the experience. Because of my thinking, those religious people who are pro-life categorize me as pro-choice. I wish I could convince them that I am really a *pro-lover* who is much more interested in loving people than in judging them.

We have defined enough. Let's look at where the New Testament supports, both outwardly and subtly, the ethics of Jesus.

"I give you a new commandment, that you love one another. Just as I have loved you, you should also love one another. By this everyone will know that you are my disciples, if you have love for one another." Jesus in John 13:34-35

❧

"One should forgive one's enemies...but not until after they're hanged." Heinrich Heine (I have no idea who he is or where I found this but, I know his axiom is the sentiment of too many people. It certainly isn't the ethics of Jesus.)

CHAPTER 6

JESUS AND HIS FRIENDS TALK ABOUT LOVE

A ten year old joined the church so that he could get a bike. He had heard that if one has enough faith and prays hard, they will receive whatever they want. He found the passage in Scriptures: "Ask and it will be given to you." (Matthew 7:7). He kept praying and praying but no bike was forthcoming. After many months of asking, he finally figured it out. He stole the bike and asked for forgiveness. (Please do not try this at home. It will not work.)

This could be a rather boring chapter if I simply quote, over and over, chapter and verse(s) all the places in the Gospels that Jesus and his friends talk about love and his ethics either directly or indirectly. I don't want to put you to sleep in two minutes, so what I would like to do is choose certain passages, which I feel best exemplify Jesus' ethics.

Let us start with one of the more popular parables, the Prodigal Son[1]. It's the story of a father who gives his young son his inheritance. The son goes out, squanders it and ends up living in a pigpen, which is not a good place for Jewish people to live. The son then decides to go home and beg for another chance, if only to have a roof over his head. His Dad sees him returning and welcomes him with open arms and prepares a huge feast. It is at this point when I wonder what my reaction would be if one of our daughters were to go off, spend all her money (really our money), dishonor the family name and disgrace herself? Would I greet her with open arms? Would I reject her? ("You made your bed. Now lie in it.") Would there be a lecture and a punishment before I would allow her to return? If I really believe in the ethics of Jesus, then I would need to emulate the father in the parable. He accepted his errant son as he was, forgave him immediately and loved him unconditionally.

Does that mean that he forgave and forgot? I suspect not. I would not be surprised if after all the dust settled, Dad didn't sit down with his son and have a heart to heart conversation about what happened. Perhaps he told him, "I forgive you son, but I shall never forget what you did." It was probably devastating to the father. What he did, was to forgive and move on with life. Did he immediately trust his boy? I hope not. Perhaps he made his youngest work very hard at regaining the trust of the whole family. Not necessarily an easy task. I would imagine that he made it very clear to his son that he had to start at the bottom of the ladder and work his way up into a position of trust. He probably also made it very clear to his prodigal that he had spent his inheritance, and there would be no more. But all this was done in the name of *agape,* unconditional love. This is the behavior we must emulate if we are to be followers. This is a behavior that goes way beyond the call of duty.

Sometimes, part two of this parable is forgotten. It's about the older son who wanted to make his useless brother suffer. He had no concept of unconditional love. He was livid that his father had shown his brother unconditional love, had been so accepting, so forgiving. That older brother can be "us." But Jesus is saying, in my Kingdom, only unconditional love prevails. As believers we have to do it Jesus' way. This is not always easy.

The next parable I would like to use as an example is The Good Samaritan.[2] The story has much more power if one understands the long held bitter dispute between the Jews and the Samaritans. This dispute had gone on since 722 BCE. The Samaritans felt they were the true children of Yahweh. They had their own version of Judaism, and had even constructed their own temple. Jews and Samaritans were bitter enemies. Jesus tells lots of stories about Samaritans, and if one reads between the lines, one can sense that Jesus was very aware of this antagonism and perhaps had some of it himself. After all, he was raised in this atmosphere. With that understanding, the power of the story is more poignant because of the *agape* love shown by the Samaritan.

I think it is interesting that the priest (obviously Jewish) did not want to have anything to do with the man who was also Jewish. It was also one of those little pokes that Jesus liked to take at the Jewish priesthood. The Levite, an order of the Judaic priesthood, also passed by this seriously wounded countryman. This was yet another dig by Jesus at the religious hierarchy. The Samaritan, "the enemy," comes along and not only gives aid but also takes the man to an inn, prepays the innkeeper and promises to pay more if needed. This is *agape*, the love of a neighbor, a so-called adversary, but is also a great story about forgiveness. Jesus wants us to rise to this level of love in which acceptance and forgiveness are paramount.

Could you do this? We shall never *really* know how we are going to behave, until we are faced with the situation. In the meantime, it is important to listen to the parable again and again so that this sort of behavior becomes deeply ingrained in our being. Then it will become natural behavior.

I could exegete (to interpret a text) the many other parables, but I don't think that is necessary. Most of them are about *agape* love either directly or indirectly. Let me switch gears and discuss what Jesus had to say, or do, about other components of *agape.*

Acceptance is a key component of *agape* and is not always easy to do. What is your reaction when you see a homeless man/woman coming toward you? How do you feel about fundamentalists, all kinds? Should we lock them up and throw away the key? What would happen if a pedophile moved into your neighborhood? Suppose a prostitute were to confront you on the street? Are you uncomfortable around people with mental or physical disabilities? Where do you stand with accepting *everyone* as a neighbor? The ethics of Jesus say we have to.

How good was Jesus at accepting people who were not Jewish or Jewish outcasts? First, let me share this. I do not believe that all the stories in Scripture are true. They are not historical facts. They were never intended to be so. Some of the stories might not contain an iota of a true fact, but they all represent a truth as perceived by the author. Some Biblical scholars call Scriptures religious history as opposed to factual history. All histories have a bias. The author interprets as best he can, coming from his point of view. Stories about Jesus have the bias of the author and many, if not most, narratives about Jesus are not necessarily factual. But one can find truth in them.

Let me share an example of a well-known Bible story, which represents a religious history. I was reading in the newspaper that some people are claiming to have found the long lost Garden of Eden in Iraq. As I read the story I chuckled. There is no actual place called the Garden of Eden. That story is a myth full of the truth, which essentially is this: Most humanity knows the difference between right and wrong, but because we live in freedom, we have a choice. Sometimes we eat of the "forbidden fruit" (please note the word "apple" is never used in the story) and then have to pay the price, as did Adam and Eve. Today, the figurative Garden of Adam and Eve [3] is still very much with us. Just read your daily newspaper or watch the 6 o'clock news.

They are full of today's version of the figurative Garden of Eden. The Bible, both the Old and New Testament, is religious history where the facts are not nearly as important as a truth found in the story.

I share this because it is important for me to let you, the reader, know that I do not necessarily believe that Jesus actually did some of these things attributed to him. The story from the Gospel of John, 4th Chapter[4] is one of them. It demonstrates how Jesus accepted those whom his own religion would not accept, a Samaritan and a woman who had been married many times. I doubt this ever actually happened, but I believe strongly in the message. It is often referred to as Jesus and the woman at the well. He and his followers were going through Samaria on their way to Galilee. Remember, there was no love lost between the Samaritans and the rest of the Jews. The disciples had gone to buy food and Jesus was alone at a well, thirsty, but without the means to draw water from the well. It was noon and the sun was at its peak. A woman appeared and Jesus asked her for a drink. She couldn't believe it. Not only was she a Samaritan being spoken to by a Jew, but also a woman. Men did not speak to women in public. The story is a bit convoluted for me, but the truth is there, Jesus holds the key to living life to its fullest. It is all about love. I share the story because it is a wonderful example of Jesus accepting people regardless of who they are. He broke three cultural barriers. The first, he spoke to a woman, second, to a woman who had been married five times and the third being that she was a hated Samaritan.

Here is another example of Jesus' acceptance of the so-called lepers of society. Jews despised tax collectors, for a variety of reasons. First, they were collecting taxes for the Romans whom the Jews also despised. Not only did they occupy the sacred land of the Jews, but they also brutalized them. The tax collectors were protected by the Roman military and that gave them license to cheat their own people. The Jews ostracized them from their society. They were scorned. Then along came Jesus, who accepted them as they were. His close friend and disciple Matthew was a tax collector. There was also Levi.[5] The story of Zaccheaus is one of my favorites.[6] He was a little man (in stature), the chief tax collector, very rich and disliked. Jesus ended up in his home and because of Jesus' acceptance of him he changed his life. This is the power of love and acceptance.

Lepers in the time of Jesus were outcasts. Once diagnosed with some kind, any kind, of skin disease (not necessarily leprosy) that person was ostracized from society and shunned by all Jews. They were forced to live like beggars outside the walls of the city, and they were not to come close to or touch "clean" people. If they did, they were killed. Jesus not only accepted them, but he touched them, which was also forbidden by law.[7]

Adultery in the time of Jesus was punishable by death for both the man and the woman. Men usually escaped the death penalty, but women, because they were simply property, were killed. One of my favorite stories appears in John. Again, I am not convinced that this incident really happened, but the punch line is a classic. The story tells us that a woman was caught committing adultery and the religious leaders were ready to stone her to death. They brought the woman to Jesus and asked him what he would do? (They were testing him one more time hoping to entrap him.) I love this part. As they were questioning him he knelt down in the sand and started doodling. Then he stood up, looked them straight in the eye, and said, "Let anyone among you who is without sin be the first to cast a stone at her." Then he knelt in the sand again and "they went away, one by one, beginning with the elders." [8] This saying is one of the mainstays of my faith: Who am I to cast a stone at anyone?

I have no idea where I found this line, but I like it: "As followers, we are asked to cross boundaries and not construct them." Sometimes I think that too often Christians feel it is their duty to build boundaries rather than cross them. Some examples might be setting up boundaries against those with alternative lifestyles, divorcees, the disabled, Jews, illegal immigrants, Roman Catholics, eastern religions, racism and the poor.

As a Christian, I am to love people, not judge them. This is not any easy thing to do. All day long we are making judgments. It is how we survive. Whether I am driving, conversing with someone, walking in a dark secluded spot, reading a story in the newspaper, looking at TV or people watching, I am making judgments. Then I am told by my religion that I am not to judge. This is a rather contradictory message. On the one hand, for survival, I have to continually make judgments. On the other hand, I hear that it is wrong. I think Jesus helps me with an answer. It is utopian, but I need to continually strive to live up to his saying found in both Matthew (7:3-5) and Luke (6:41-42). "Why do you see the speck that is in the eye of your brother but do not notice the log that is in your own eye? Or how can you say to your brother, 'Let me take the speck out of your eye' when there is a log in your own eye? You hypocrite, first take the log out of your own eye, then you will see clearly to take the speck out of your brother's eye." (Matthew) This always pulls me back from being too judgmental about others, because for the majority of my life, I have been trying to remove the log out of my own eye. I know some of the log is still there. It's at this point that I need to bring myself back to the center, the ethics of Jesus: I am to love and accept, not judge and reject. (My wife helps me with little comments like, "That's rather judgmental!")

Let us look at Jesus' ideas about forgiveness, a heady issue. In my years as a clergyperson and psychotherapist, there was one issue that kept raising its ugly head over and over. It was called forgiveness or lack thereof. People will hang on to hate, anger, and animosity for long periods of time, even a lifetime. There are some interesting points about *not* forgiving:

1. People who center their lives on revenge, hatred, anger seem to have a difficult time moving on with their lives. Their obsession consumes a great deal of time.

2. Often this will result in either physical or mental illness, which immobilizes them even further.
3. All this is caused by someone giving tremendous power to the human being they probably detest the most in life. In a sense, the unforgiven rules their life. Probably the last thing they want to happen.
4. All this negativity alienates them from friends, family, children and anyone within earshot because people become tired of hearing about ancient history.

I think Jesus knew this, not as a clergyperson or psychotherapist, but as a humanist. Over and over again he healed people by simply forgiving them. The first story that comes to mind is about the paralytic whose friends brought him to Jesus on a stretcher. The home where Jesus was speaking was packed with people, so the four friends removed the roof and lowered the paralytic down to Jesus. Matthew 9:1-8, Mark 2:1-12 and Luke 5:17-26 all tell a similar story. [9] Jesus sees him and says, "Take heart my son; your sins are forgiven…Rise, take up your bed and go home." And the man did just that. That is the power of forgiving and being forgiven. Jesus did this over and over. Forgiveness heals both the forgiver and the forgiven. Forgiving – others and oneself - is one of the cornerstones of the ethics of Jesus.

Who can forget the story about Peter asking Jesus, "Lord, how often shall my brother sin against me, and I forgive him? As many as seven times?" Jesus said to him, "I do not say to you seven times, but seventy times seven."[10] Do you realize how many times that is? It means an infinite number of times. Ouch!

The next shocker is that we are to forgive our enemies. That is a novel, creative idea. Listen to what Jesus told us, "You have heard that it was said, 'You shall love your neighbor and hate your enemies.' But I say to you, love your enemies, pray for those who persecute you." (Matthew 7:43-44). Luke (6:35) expands upon this theme as Jesus tells us,

"But love your enemies, and do good, and lend, expecting nothing in return." This is love at its highest form. It is important to add here that there is a great difference between "like" and "love." We are told to love. Nothing is said about "liking." This point can be confusing because we think that we are to like the enemy. If your spouse runs off with someone at the office, you probably consider them both the enemy. That part is fine. You probably don't like them. Nothing is wrong with that. But the ethics of Jesus tell us that you must love them, which includes forgiving and accepting them, in spite of themselves, no matter what they did to you. This will free you up so that you can move on with your life. But you do *not* have to like them. For some people this is very difficult. But it is essential if we are to lead life to its fullest.

What happens if we do not buy into forgiving? Jesus tells this challenging parable entitled, "The Unmerciful Servant."[11] A servant of a king owed the king lots of money and he was not making his monthly payments. The king then gave the orders that he, his family and all his possessions were to be sold into slavery. The servant pleaded for another chance. The king gave it to him. But then that servant went to someone who owed him a small amount of money, and demanded that he return his debt immediately. When the money was not forthcoming, the servant had him put into prison. The king heard about it, became furious and had the servant thrown into prison. The story concludes with these words from Jesus, "So also my heavenly Father will do to every one of you, if you don't forgive your brother from your heart." (Matthew 18:35)

I don't like threats like this one - God will get you. Also I also don't believe there will be a judgment day when everyone has to account for his past, so I find the final statement a bit difficult to swallow. Unless someone is a psychopath, my feelings are that when we make a mistake our major punishment is that we are forced to live with ourselves. That isn't easy. I am still in pain about something that happened when I was 19. I was playing sports for my college and had a scholarship to do so. One day, when I thought I was all alone and no one would see me, I left the fraternity house finishing a cigarette. My lacrosse coach saw me from a distance. At practice that day he told me he had seen me and told me to run 20 laps around a three quarter mile track. I lied to him and denied it vehemently. Finally, he told me it was up to me. I did not run the 20 laps. To this day (54 years later), I still feel badly that I had lied and subsequently have run hundreds of laps, but the guilt never goes away entirely. There are some other incidents in my life about which I have the same aftermath. I have forgiven myself and moved on, but those old guilt feelings linger. I do not need to stand in front of an imaginary god (like some man up there in heaven) or saint (i.e., Peter) for further punishment. I have done it to myself. I bet you could tell the same sort of story or stories.

I hope at this point you have an idea about the concept of *agape* love that Jesus promoted. A suggestion: Reread the four Gospels with the idea that they are really about *love*, not necessarily about crucifixion and resurrection.

Now let's take a look at what some of the books of the New Testament say about *agape*. This could give us some indication just whether Jesus' message about love reached the early church.

JESUS' FRIENDS TALK ABOUT LOVE

We have looked at what Jesus did and said about love. It was a powerful message in his ministry and life. The question we would like to research is: Did this message come through to the next generation? Did the early church promote the concept of loving self, neighbor and creation? The answers to these questions can be found in the letters written after Jesus' death, most of which were written before the Gospels.

Although Paul was not a personal friend of Jesus', he felt he knew Jesus personally. Before Paul converted, he worked for the so-called "FBI" of the religious leadership of

Judaism. It was his job to investigate this new Jewish schism started by a man called Jesus, from the town of Nazareth. As a result, he probably knew a great deal about "the enemy." He would have to have heard the stories about Jesus to understand his so-called heresies. He must have heard the love message over and over. Maybe it even was that message that was responsible for his conversion. Did Paul, then as a follower, promulgate that message? Many see Paul as the architect of Christianity. Later in his ministry, he placed a great deal of emphasis on Crucifixion and Resurrection theology. Although he understood the love message of Jesus, his forte was developing the concept of Jesus being the sacrificial lamb for our sins. I am uncomfortable with this concept because I am not into sin, guilt, self-loathing, guilt, expiation, guilt, judgment, guilt, etc. The strongest message from Jesus is about love, not sin. Paul knew that and stated so in his writings.

Paul's earliest letters were thought to be the first and second letters to the Thessalonians, possibly written about 52 CE. At this stage in Paul's theology, he was very sure that the second coming was right around the corner, so pack your bags folks and be ready. Obviously, it didn't happen. In I Thessalonians, he does share the idea that we are "taught by God to love one another." (4:9) Paul had the message. He knew that the Ten Commandments were the foundation of Judaism and that there were an additional 613 laws that had been developed to clarify them. But he also seemed to understand that love was the important message, more important than the law.

It was probably Jesus' disregard for the law that was partly responsible for his death. It was Jesus' contention that over the centuries the law had become more important than love. He went back to the Old Testament, Deuteronomy and Leviticus, to show his people that Judaism was about love. This was a very threatening message to the leadership who had spent their lives learning about the law and how to interpret it. Were the law to be eliminated or replaced by love, they perhaps felt their jobs would be threatened. So let's get rid of the messenger.

Jesus was and is about love, not buildings, power, money and more laws. I think Paul knew that love was Jesus' basic message. One only has to read the "Love chapter" in I Corinthians 13[12] to realize that he had a real understanding about *agape*. I use this passage at baptisms, marriages, funerals and any occasion I can fit it in because it is what followers understand: "and now faith, hope and love abide, these three; and the greatest of these is love." (I Corinthians 13:13) How can one say it any better than that?

Paul knew forgiveness was essential if one was to love self, others and God. In his letter to the Colossians (if Paul even wrote it), perhaps written while Paul was in prison in the 60s CE, he (or the author) states, "Bear with one another…forgive each other; just as the Lord has forgiven you, you must also forgive. Above all, clothe yourself with love…" (3:13) This is the ethics of Jesus moving through the early church. Unfortunately, along the way Paul started making Jesus into something I don't think Jesus ever considered, such as being the sacrificial lamb, the perfect sin offering, the propitiation (the appeaser) for our sins, starting from the "original" one. It is at this stage in the early church that we start to see the Crucifixion/Resurrection theology push the love message of Jesus into the background.

I have a problem with this. We are told God is love. We are children of God. We are loved by God. Then the church turns around and tells us we were born bad (Original Sin), out of relationship with God. As the popular hymn "Amazing Grace" reminds us all the time, we are "wretches." ("Amazing grace, how sweet the sound that saved a wretch like me.") I don't consider myself a wretch nor do I consider most people wretches. We are Creatures of Creation, which signifies good to me. But I have this feeling that the church is afraid that if they tell people they are good, they will stop coming.

I don't have any problem with a Resurrection theology as long as one doesn't take it literally. For me, it is a figurative concept and applies to each of our lives. We have all had our Good Fridays, and Jesus, with his ethics based on love, can help us turn that Good Friday experience (figurative Crucifixion) into an Easter (Resurrection) experience. Paul puts it this way, "No longer present your members to sin as instruments of wickedness, but present yourselves to God as instruments of righteousness" (Romans 6:13).

The Letter to the Romans is Paul's most advanced theology, written before he went to Rome, probably in the late 50s CE. In it, he has a great deal to say about love and its components. One idea of Paul's that I find interesting is that the law enslaves us. We are so busy obeying the law (we're enslaved) that we forget to love. In Romans 10:4, we read, "For Christ is the end of the law so that there may be righteousness for everyone who believes." Romans 6:6, "We know that our old self was crucified with him so that the body of sin (known through the law) might be destroyed, and we might no longer be enslaved to sin." We become slaves to obeying laws whether they make sense or not. So many feel that by obeying the law they will become perfect. The Episcopal church tries to tell me that I must obey their laws and authority or face dire circumstances, maybe even being defrocked. This church has told me that I cannot bless any union between people of the same sex. I disagree, vehemently. If the Church is about love, then everyone is equal. Our country says, "Liberty and justice for all," unless you happen to have an alternative life style. Then you become a second-class citizen. There is no way I can justify that with the ethics of Jesus.

I love this statement of Paul's in his letter to the Galatians, probably written in the late 50s CE. "For the whole law is summed up in a single commandment, "You shall love your neighbor as yourself" (5:14). A little later in the chapter he shares, "The fruit of the Spirit is love, joy, peace, patience, kindness, generosity, faithfulness, gentleness and self-control" (5:22). I appreciate the words of a theologian concerning this passage: "Doctrinal orthodox without the active manifestation of love is not the faith of which Paul speaks." (The author is unknown to me.) Nor is it the faith about which Jesus spoke.

I think Paul is written proof that the early church understood the main message of Jesus. In Romans (12:20), Paul repeats the words of Jesus: "If your enemies are hungry, feed them. If they are thirsty, give them something to drink." In Matthew 25:35, Jesus said the same thing. I see this passage (Matthew 25:31-46) entitled "The Last Judgment," as one of the most important passages in the New Testament. [13] Essentially, Jesus is telling us that unless we as followers feed the hungry, clothe the poor, visit the sick and those in prison, welcome strangers, we are not carrying out his wishes or doing his work. No place in this passage do I see anything about building buildings, collecting offerings so they can pay themselves, developing elaborate rituals and making a multitude of rules. The church needs to concentrate on doing love.

Let us take a fast look at what a few others in the early church said about the subject. James wrote one letter. One is not sure if the author is the brother of Jesus, or the brother of John, or the son of Alphaeus, or a pretender, someone claiming to be James. Whoever it is, the author of James 2:8 reminds us, "You do well if you really fulfill the royal law according to the scripture, 'You shall love your neighbor as yourself.'" This is proof that the ethics of Jesus had survived.

Peter, either the original or another "pretender," wrote two letters, probably in the early 60s CE. In his first letter (4:8), the author tells us, "Above all, maintain constant love for one another, for love covers a multitude of sins."

John, again either a pretender or apostle or maybe the author of the gospel by the same name or perhaps even the author of that first century science-fiction fantasy, The Book of Revelation, wrote three letters. In his first letter, John hits the nail on the head when he tells us, "Little children, let us love, not in word or speech, but in truth and action." (3:18) This quote is a marvelous segue into our next chapter, the meat of this book.

"...a lawyer stood up to put him to the test, saying, 'Teacher, what shall I do to inherit eternal life?' He said to him, 'What is written in the law? How do you read?' And he answers, 'You shall love the Lord your God with all your heart, and with all your soul, and with all your strength, and with all your mind; and your neighbor as yourself.' And Jesus said to him, 'You have answered right; do this and you will live.'" (Luke 10:25-28)

CHAPTER 7:

PUTTING THE ETHICS OF JESUS INTO ACTION

I found an old tattered yellowed "Non Sequitur" comic strip that I had saved for years. Moses was standing at the base of the mountain where he had just received The Ten Commandments. He was positioned behind the lectern, pointing to the commandments. The crowd is in front of him raising their arms frantically hoping their question would be recognized next. The caption reads, "I believe that the leaving-the-toilet-seat-up would be covered under both commandments four and five...next question."

We have, in the previous six chapters, been building a case suggesting that the primary message from Jesus was about love. Not any kind of love but the highest kind, *agape*. Not necessarily an easy love to put into practice because one must understand the concept before using it successfully. In no way is it going to fit neatly in between "the fourth and fifth commandments." At times, with the ethics of Jesus, (based on *agape)* "leaving-the-toilet-seat-up" would be the proper thing to do. At other times, depending on the circumstances, the toilet seat must go down.

Before we begin looking at the *Standards* or the basis of the ethics of Jesus, allow me to first share some ideas that I hope might help clarify the Standards.

AGAPE LOVE IS NOT ABOUT "LIKING"

This might be a difficult clarification. Many people envision Jesus as a "Mr. Nice Guy." He loved everyone and everyone loved him. I don't believe this for a minute. Jesus did not like some of the religious leaders, especially as they tried to entrap him. He seemed to be at odds with them most of the time. He did not like the rich young man who wanted Jesus to give him the key to living a fuller life. Jesus then told him to sell all his possessions and give the proceeds to the poor. The man could not do this. One has the feeling that this young man truly disappointed Jesus because he was so in love with his money. Jesus did not really like Samaritans. For centuries there had been great animosity between Jews and Samaritans. There are more examples, but the point is, in spite of who they were or what they did, Jesus loved them all. His standard was to love, not necessarily like, all humanity.

When I was living in Hawai'i and working on the Bishop's staff, I had an office on the second floor of the cathedral's administrative building. I often worked after hours and would be the only clergy in the building. The cathedral in Honolulu was downtown and there were many homeless. Regularly they would "hit" the cathedral staff for money, so I became a candidate. I could hear them coming. They would stick their head in my office, bless me and start in with their story. After I had heard enough story I would ask, "How can I help you?" "Oh Father, I haven't eaten for three days. My government check is coming in two days and I need some money to tide me over." "I need bus money to get me to ____________ (sometimes it was even the

Mainland) where there was going to be a job, money, help, etc."

Now I really didn't like these people. They smelled, were often dirty, would lie to me and try to con me out of cash. For this reason, I did not carry much money, just a few dollars. But I did have plenty of coupons. I would ask them, "Do you want a meal? Here's a coupon for a restaurant." "Here's a bus ticket." If they had a car story then, "Here's a gas voucher for $5." "Here's a voucher for a room." Most of them did not want what they were requesting. They wanted only cold hard cash, which I knew would be spent for some kind of drug. Most of the time they left empty-handed, sometimes cursing me goodbye. Even though I did not like them, I loved them simply as fellow human beings. I offered them help if they truly wanted the help they requested. This is like versus love.

If we are honest with ourselves there are probably more people out there (and maybe even some in our own family) we don't like. But we must love them.

TOUGH LOVE

Let us look at "tough love," which often does not have a great deal of like in it. It is a love that confronts people with the truth, as painful as it might be, and some sort of action perceived by the receiver as being negative. Let us talk about the 25-year old son who is into drugs, still lives at home, does not work and is abusive to his parents. They tell him he must be out of the house in 24 hours and not to return until he is sober and in a program. The son becomes abusive, the parents call the police, have him arrested, put in jail and leave him there. That's tough love.

People do not see Jesus as someone who doled out tough love. There are people who feel that Jesus was too nice a person (after all he was God) to confront others with truth. This myth is squelched when you see him deal with some people. His confrontations were not only with the religious leadership, but also his best friends and even his family.

Early in his ministry, Jesus returned to Nazareth and taught in the synagogue (Luke 4:16-19). He was not well received. "They took offense at him." (Mark 6:57) Then some of the villagers wanted to kill him, but he disappeared and, for a period of time, would have nothing to do with his immediate family.[1] He felt rejected by them.

Then there is the story about when Jesus was preaching and his mother and some of his family came to talk with him. Someone told Jesus, "his mother and brothers stood outside, asking to speak to him." (Matthew 12:46-50). Jesus then publicly rejected his family and told the crowds, "Whoever does the will of my Father in heaven is my brother, and sister, and mother." (Matthew 12:50) Again, Jesus rejected his hostile family. That is tough love.

Agape demands tough love as well as tender, caring love, whether we like the person or not!

PREJUDICE

One of my own self-inventories has been to develop a list of people or groups toward whom I have a prejudice, for whatever reason. I know it is wrong to have prejudices, but as a human being, I know that I make judgments about others and that I have prejudices. Often, this is how we survive. For example, if we are walking down the street and we see a dirty, unkempt man mumbling to himself staggering toward us, what are we going to do? We need to make some quick judgments: Are we going to continue walking toward him? Or are we going to get out of his way? Some of these judgments are based on past experience; some are based simply on feelings, uncomfortable ones. Our prejudices come to the surface. Perhaps there are many, such as the color of his skin, or the fact that he is filthy dirty, or maybe mentally unbalanced or inebriated or he could be violent. We don't know how he is going to react toward us and we feel uneasy. All that is normal. However, what makes prejudices unacceptable is not that we have prejudices, but that our prejudices control us. Do my prejudices prevent me from helping this homeless man or anyone else? I would hope not, but I do admit that in situations like this my prejudices show up and help rule my decisions. But at this point, I need to put my prejudice behind me and love that person.

We need to deal with our prejudices (which every human being has) creatively, so that they do not get in the way of our being able to help others.

LOVE AND INDIFFERENCE

A long time ago I learned that the opposite of love is not hate, it is indifference. Most of us have an understanding about hate, but indifference is sneaky. One is not quite sure when a person is being indifferent. We perceive someone as quiet and aloof. We can say to ourselves, maybe that person is not feeling well or got up on the wrong side of the bed. On the other hand, they could be very angry with us. We ask them if they are angry with us and they say, "Oh no!" Then we ask them what is wrong and they respond, "Oh nothing." But we still feel a tension and now it becomes obvious that we are not going to get the truth from the other person. This is how indifference works. It leaves the receiver up in the air.

Do you want to get rid of your significant other and come out like the good guy? Be indifferent to him/her and then deny it. It will drive the other person crazy! Indifference kills just as much as hate and has no place in the ethics of Jesus.

BEWARE OF YOUR CONSCIENCE! IT SHOULD NOT BE YOUR GUIDE

So that we have a common understanding, let me define conscience: "The inner sense of what is right or wrong in one's conduct or motive." (Random House Unabridged Dictionary)

I was raised in a Christian household. My father was a clergyman and my mother a saint. They were straight arrows who led an exemplary life instilling the highest sense of values, not only in our family, but also in our extended family. It was from my parents that I developed my set of values, which were reasonably well instilled by the time I was five years old. Unfortunately, their values and the ethics of Jesus were different. They did not necessarily accept everyone, fully. It was subtle, but it was there, the racism, sexism, homophobia, elitism among other "isms." This was how my conscience was developed. I did not even know that I had subtle prejudices until I encountered the ethics of Jesus. Then I realized that I too had all these little "isms" that prohibited me from fully accepting people because I would judge people based on my "conscience." Here are examples of some of the subtle lessons I learned from my parents.

- Jews did kill Jesus. Watch out when dealing with them. They are crafty.
- It was acceptable that women were nurses, secretaries and school teachers, but they could never be a priest in the Episcopal church or President of the United States.
- It was fine that blacks lived a mile away and that a few attended our church. But do not let them move any closer.
- We recognize that a few people might be homosexual or "effeminate" (the subject could never be an open discussion 60 years ago), but we hope our son is not one of those.
- In the 1940s when we were at war with the Germans, Italians and Japanese, I had some choice words when referring to them. They were derogatory but that was disguised as patriotism. It was acceptable to call the Japanese "Japs" or "Nips." No one ever reprimanded me for using those terms. The war ended, but that did not necessarily end my usage of choice words. At the age of eighteen, here is what my conscience told me.
  - "Japs" were sneaky.
  - Of course the Jews killed Jesus, so I had my negative words for Jewish people.

- Living in a black neighborhood, as a youth, I had my run-ins with them. They bullied me, so I had another set of choice words for them.
- I did not know any openly gay (we did not even use this term back in those days) people, because a gay person would not admit it publicly. But I still had awful things and terrible words to say about them because I had learned that gay people were bad. They were all pedophiles who would try to "convert" me.
- All Germans are Nazis, and it was acceptable to call them "krauts"!
- God only loved Christians, except for the Roman Catholics. They were papists and wrong. After all, they had murdered all those people during the Inquisition.
- I was to obey my parents no matter what. The Bible told me so.
- There were no alcoholics among nice people. Only the bums who lived in or by the gutter were alcoholics.
- Bad criminals needed to be "fried" in the electric chair.

I could go on about the people my *conscience* told me would not be acceptable, but I believe the point has been made. Even with what I thought was a Christian conscience, there were quite a few individuals and/or groups whom I had discounted.

Who are the people in your mind/conscience for whom you have negative feelings? This is an inventory all believers need to go through so that we can be aware of those toward whom we have predisposed feelings. We need to constantly check our conscience against the ethics of Jesus because the two could clash.

LOVE AND JUSTICE ARE THE SAME BECAUSE JUSTICE (MORAL) IS LOVE DISTRIBUTED

In the above clarification we are talking about *agape* and moral justice as opposed to legal justice. The latter is the law that each society establishes as being the law of the land. Moral justice is giving every human being his or her due. It makes no difference about their color, creed and economic status; each human being is to enjoy the same love/justice.

Let me try an example: In our "Pledge of Allegiance" we state, over and over, "liberty and justice for all." This statement is moral justice. In reality, that is not the way it works. Ask the poor, the homeless, the uneducated or undereducated, blacks, gays, lesbians, Hispanics, the disabled, ex-convicts, just to mention a few, if, in this country, we provide liberty and justice for all? It's a redundant question. All the above-mentioned people are second, some even third, class citizens. In many places in our country we even have laws guaranteeing that some of the above-mentioned folks will not ever enjoy moral justice. Having money, an education, political power or influence opens doors that are not available to many in the United States. Thus, the moral justice of "liberty and justice for all" becomes "legal justice" which is not always just.

I do believe that all societies need a semblance of order and that the law is the best method to provide this. But in the process there are some laws that are ridiculous and some that are anti-*agape*. Because I am a believer in the ethics of Jesus I have a moral responsibility to oppose and change those laws. I watch Jesus as he opposed the religious leaders and their laws. Luke 6:1-11[2] tells of two incidences of Jesus breaking the Jewish rules about the Sabbath. The first has to do with the disciples going through the grain-fields picking and eating grain on the Sabbath. This was a "no-no" for Jews and some Pharisees questioned Jesus about what his disciples were doing. Jesus gave them an example of the great King David doing the same and then told them, "The Son of man is lord of the Sabbath." I see this as a subtle way of Jesus telling us that *agape* was more important than any law.

On another Saturday (Sabbath) Jesus healed a man with a withered hand, right in front of some Pharisees. They were livid. Jews did not heal people on the Sabbath, but Jesus thumbed his proverbial nose at the silliness of this law. The man was there and needed healing. There are many more examples of how Jesus demonstrated that moral justice is the ruling norm and his ethics takes precedence over legal law.

Legal justice always threatens to suffocate and cheat moral justice. If we really believe in liberty and justice for all, then there would be absolutely no issue with full rights for people with other lifestyles than heterosexual. But you have some of the leadership of such groups as the Religious Right, The Moral Majority, most Christian fundamentalists/ evangelicals, Roman Catholics, just to mention a few, who want to pass a constitutional amendment that marriage can only be between a man and a woman. Obviously, this is aimed at the gay/lesbian community to make certain they remain second class citizens who cannot enjoy the rights and privileges of the heterosexual members of this country. Any law against any group of people in the United States is unconstitutional, immoral and opposed to the ethics of Jesus. If such a law were to pass in the USA, I believe love would demand that there be some kind of revolution.

It has happened before, many times. The start of our country was about just that. The Boston Tea Party is a wonderful example of how *agape* must revolt when the law starts infringing on the basic rights of human beings. Non-violently, a small group of men boarded English ships and threw the cargo of tea into the bay rather than pay exorbitant taxes demanded by the king. The colonists would not tolerate the idea of taxation without representation. No one was hurt and the message quickly went back to England that the people in this colony wanted representation. Justice was served and no one was hurt.

THE ETHICS OF JESUS VERSUS RESURRECTION THEOLOGY

I have attempted to show that the main message of Jesus was/is about love. In my estimation, this message has been clouded by the stories involving Crucifixion and Resurrection. Admittedly, in the Good Friday and Easter stories the concept of love has been quietly woven into these events. Orthodox theology has told us that God loved/loves us so much that he allowed *His* Son to die on the Cross for us, wretched, miserable sinners that we are. I have a difficult time with all these concepts. First, it makes God a man. I find this most limiting when one considers the vastness of the universe. Next, the idea that this "man up there" has a son also reeks of anthropomorphism. To make matters worse, this son is born of a virgin. This is humanly impossible. The church declared Jesus a *total human* in the fourth century (531 CE) at the Council of Ephesus. Total human beings do not come from virgins. (See Chapter 2, "Theologically Speaking…") Since Jesus supposedly is the one and only Son of God, it would be logical to assume he had no human father. Yet, some of the gospels tell us that Joseph was Jesus' father.[3] The idea that Joseph was Jesus' "earthly father" (versus God as heavenly Father) just compounds the absurdity.

Next, if I am to believe in an historical Jesus, a man who really existed, there can be no such thing as a physical resurrection. It is humanly impossible, especially considering the physical damage (nails through his hands and feet, a spear jabbed into his side) that was done to Jesus. It is very difficult to logically believe that Jesus, after being declared dead by the centurion, would wake up and be physically there. (Please! No rebuttal with "God can do anything!" It countermands the church's teaching about free will, predestination and freedom.)

Finally, as I have stated before, I do not believe that all human beings are wretched sinners for whom someone needs to die. We all miss the mark occasionally but I think people are basically good and don't need someone to die for them. They need someone to show them ways to do life better. Jesus does that for me.

We are now going to look at the four basic Standards of Jesus' ethics. They are not complicated.

STANDARD 1: *Agape* love is the foundation of the ethics of Jesus; only one thing is right and good...*agape.*

As we have discussed, *agape* is a giving love, expecting nothing in return. It is the highest form of love. This is not to say that *philia, storge, eros* aren't good. It is just that *agape* is the best. The other three loves always expect something in return. There is nothing wrong with this. All three can turn into *agape*. Let us use as an example a couple has been married fifty plus years. They are friends, *philia,* who have enjoyed a mutually enjoyable sex life, *eros,* but then she has a severe heart attack and is left partially paralyzed, incontinent and with a damaged brain that has a difficult time speaking and remembering. At this point, the *philia/eros* is going to become *agape.* Her husband expects nothing in return because he realizes that his wife is not capable of giving much more than half smiles and perhaps a feeble hand squeeze. Over and over we are called upon as followers to give, expecting nothing in return.

We have the freedom and, if you believe in the ethics of Jesus, the responsibility to do *agape.* Our lives need to be centered on the concept of constantly striving to love. Sometimes the most loving thing to do is not always the thing society suggests. It could result in such behavior as telling lies, committing suicide, killing someone, stealing, doing something illegal, disobeying authority and maybe even committing adultery. More about this in a bit.

Remember: *Agape* is the foundation of Jesus' ethics.

<u>STANDARD 2</u>: *Agape* must include acceptance of ourselves and every other human being, whether we like them or not.

Here is a difficult question: "Do you love you?" Many folks are offended by such a question, primarily because in our society we think self-love/narcissism is wrong. We call it conceit and generally people do not appreciate someone who is conceited. In my classes, when the above question is asked, some become defensive, others remain silent. They are afraid to respond and say to themselves, "I don't want to answer this question because it sounds like a lose/lose proposition. No matter what I say it will sound wrong. But this is not a book about what is socially acceptable behavior. It's about love.

As followers we must love ourselves. (I did not say like.) After all, we are creatures of Creation. We were made in the image of Creation, in the image of love. Maybe I do not like the fact that I am only 5 feet 8 inches tall and weigh 150 pounds (I really want to be 6'5" and 275 pounds of rock hard muscle), that my toes are short, that I wear quadruple EEEE size shoes and a list of other things wrong with my physical being. That is not the issue. I am certain that every human being, if they would write a wish list of all the physical changes they would like to have, it would be long. But physical traits have nothing to do with *agape* or loving ourselves.

I believe every human being has the capability to do unbelievable things with this life regardless of their physical appearance. Each of us can be an instrument to help change the world for the better. Look at Jesus, considered a peasant in his society, minimally educated, who never traveled more than 200 miles from his home, but a man who used his gifts to revolutionize the world 2,000 years ago. And he is still revolutionizing the world today. He was a human being just like you and me. He too could have had his private wish list of all the physical changes he would like to have had. But this was not important to him. Love was his primary goal and with it Jesus made unbelievable things happen, not only in his three-year ministry, but also for the past 2,000 years.

As I read the Gospels I have the feeling that Jesus loved who he was even if others did not. One can sense this idea when one observes how he dealt with all sorts and conditions of humanity. He is portrayed as being self-confident whether he was dealing with the religious leaders, lepers, tax collectors, women, his close followers or the crowds. He gave an air of being in charge. He loved his humanity.

In my years as a pastoral counselor and psychotherapist, one of the major issues I encountered was the vast number of people who did not love themselves. Some even *hated* who they were. It was and is difficult to do effective therapy with people who hate themselves. I think some psychotherapists make a great deal of money from people who hate themselves because it is a real challenge to change the mindset of those who feel they are worthless. One can keep such clients in therapy for years. Unfortunately, the institutional church does not help. Too many churches operate under the mantra that all human beings are wretched, unworthy sinners and even *miserable* sinners. Then the church talks about being perfect, which in my estimation, makes people feel even worse about themselves (See Chapter 2, **PERFECTION**) because, no matter how hard they try, they never attain that state.

Many Christians believe that Jesus was perfect, which indicates to me that they have not read the gospels in depth. If one were to read Matthew, Mark and Luke looking for the humanity of Jesus, they would soon see a fellow human being who had all the human imperfections the rest of us do. I see him as a man who, at times, lost his cool. He could be short with people. Ask the woman at the well in Samaria; or Peter, who was reminded that he was not the sharpest tack in the box. Read Matthew 23[4] where Jesus goes after, with no holds barred, the religious leaders. He called them awful things. Members of his family have no illusions about their son and brother being perfect. They thought he was a loser who was crazy. One of the reasons Jesus is my Christ is because of his humanity. I know he was not perfect and if he was, I would not be the least bit interested in him as my Christ, because he would then be some fictional character with whom I could not identify.

People who see themselves in a negative light also have a tendency to tell themselves over and over that they are incompetent, inadequate, have no talents, no skills and no gifts. They can be highly critical of others to mask their feelings of inadequacy and have a difficult time making friends because most people do not want to be with those who are so self-deprecating. When one has such feelings of worthlessness, it really makes it difficult, if not impossible, to love oneself and others.

How many times have you ever heard the institutional church tell us how wonderful we are as creatures of Creation? Unfortunately, not enough. The central message of Christianity needs to be about the innate goodness and uniqueness of every human being. It is a shame that the overpowering message of the church seems too often to be primarily about our human wretchedness.

I have said a great deal about the ethics of Jesus and his demand that we fully accept every human being. We can make judgments about others, dislike them, and make disparaging remarks, but the ethics of Jesus insist that we rise above all this and accept every human being because all of us are Creatures of Creation. I have shared with you that I am a recovering homophobic, chauvinist, racist, bigot, sexist, elitist and more. The way I rose above my prejudices centered on Jesus' standard that I must accept every human being as they are. This has freed me. Now, I do not need to make judgments or reinforce my prejudices about others. I simply need to love all my fellow humans.

As I have told you, I went to an all boys' prep school, a men's college, the male dominated Marine Corps and then a seminary with only males. My homophobia was fed at each of those places so that by the time I became a priest, it was so well entrenched that I even bought into Paul's homophobia. The ethics of Jesus forced me to reevaluate my position about people and I did a 180-degree turn.

- Now I can see clearly the importance of the gay community in the church and in society. They add a wholesome new dimension to life. Thanks to Jesus' ethic, I am a recovering homophobic.
- A street person could be you or me. We must accept them where they are and then *agape* them. Jesus reminds us, "As you did it to one of the least of these my brethren, you did it to me" (Matthew 25:40).
- Women are equal to men and bring great and unique gifts to the world. I no longer consider myself a practicing sexist or chauvinist. (Being raised in a predominately female household and having raised three daughters with two granddaughters has also helped.)
- Every religion offers beautiful and diverse points of view about creation/creator. They all consider love as their foundation. I am no longer a Christian elitist.
- Every race of humanity is made up of Creatures of Creation. My racism is under control, but I am still working on this one. The *agape* ethics of Jesus has transformed and continues to transform my life.

Unfortunately, like all converts, I probably go over the edge in my support of people with different lifestyles. Now I feel very uncomfortable with the homophobic community who, for the most part, has no willingness to listen to current relevant information about why some people are born gay. It tends to confuse their erroneous thinking. I tell people it is offensive to me for them to make disparaging remarks about others even in the form of a racist or sexist joke. I challenge the double talk of the Christian Right (called either fundamentalists or evangelicals) who say they love everyone, but then say that the lifestyle of the gay and lesbian community is a choice and a wrong one. I want nothing to do with that sort of thinking. It is foreign to the ethics of Jesus and unacceptable. I love fundamentalists, but I do not like much of their thinking or theology.

The ethics of Jesus demand that we accept ourselves and all others.

STANDARD 3: *Agape* demands that we forgive self and others immediately.

It is a toss-up: Is it easier to accept self and others or forgive self and others? One would think that if one fully accepts self and others then they have gone through a process of forgiving. But this is not necessarily true. For most humans, forgiveness is difficult. It seems to be more natural to go after "the pound of flesh." Vengeance, revenge, getting even, seems to be ingrained in us. Maybe that is why Jesus was so big on the concept of forgiveness. He realized this. He was raised in the Jewish culture with the unwritten law, "an eye for an eye and a tooth for a tooth." Forgiveness was not a foundation stone of Judaism. Obviously, Jesus disagreed. I suspect he saw the damage that being unforgiving and unforgiven could inflict on oneself and others.

At one point in my career I conducted what I called "Divorce Recovery Workshops." I think divorce is a part of life. It is not necessarily a good one, but a reality. When two people fall out of love (if they were ever in love in the first place), I see it more damaging to each of those people, their children and families if they stay in the relationship for whatever reason. So either get to work on the relationship (if *both* people are willing) and make it work or divorce and move on with life. Unfortunately, too many people do not move on and take the baggage of hate and unforgiveness with them. Is there anything more boring than a divorced person giving their litany of hate as to why they won't forgive the other person and go forward? There is an interesting dynamic that takes place here. Because "A" won't forgive "B" whom they really dislike (perhaps hate), then the very last person they would ever want to give power to, "B," now has power over them. In a sense "B" rules their life because "A" won't let go, forgive and move on. "A" seems to spend a great deal of time telling anyone who will listen how awful "B" was and is. "A" needs to get over "B" because until they do "B" rules the roost.

The next idea along these lines is that the life of "A" is consumed with wanting their pound of flesh. "A" will do everything possible to make the life of "B" miserable. That seems to be the modus operandi of "A." He or she will poison their children's minds so that the child(ren) feels guilty about having a relationship with "B." "A" will have no friends who might continue being friends with "B." Everyone must hate, detest "B." This is their life. It's a sad commentary, but until they learn that there *can* be life after divorce, they cannot start living. Forgiveness would cure this immediately because one of the biggest rewards of forgiving is that it has a releasing action for both the forgiver and the forgiven.

There is the story about Jesus forgiving the paralyzed man on a stretcher right after he got off a boat.[5] Jesus realized the man's major illness had to do with forgiveness, so he said to him, "Take heart, my son; your sins are forgiven." Some religious leaders were watching and they thought that the words and actions of Jesus were blasphemous. Jesus felt their hostility and challenged them. Then he turned to the man and said, "Rise, take your bed and go home." The man did just that: "And he rose and went home." Just by being forgiven (we do not know for what), not only is the man healed and released but he could then move on with his life.

There was an article in a magazine called "Bottom Line" (January 15, 2005) entitled, "The Healing Power of Forgiveness." It starts, "Recent studies have proven what major religions advocate - showing your antagonists compassion and letting go of the desire for revenge can improve your psychological and physical health… forgiveness lowers the risk of heart problems. Ellis Cose interviewed victims of some of the worst atrocities of our time—survivors of the Holocaust and African genocides…adults molested by priests in childhood…parents of children murdered by people now on death row…and families of those killed in the September 11th terrorist attacks. Cose was amazed at how many of these ordinary human beings found the capacity and willingness to forgive -and were better off for it." The article shared this thought: "Resentment is like drinking poison and waiting for it to kill your enemy."

I like this axiom: Forgive and move on. Forgive and forget does not work. Unless you lose your mind, the precipitating event is going to be remembered. Life is too short and precious to be hung up on the past. Real living happens at this moment and in the future. We can accomplish nothing reliving the past. It's gone. So forgive and go forward.

I have learned over the years to accept the fact that if there is an altercation with another person, I have to accept part of the responsibility. Just by "being" I have become part of the problem, whether I realized it or not. If I was not alive, there would have been no issue. Some folks really fight me on this. They feel they need to blame and to be exonerated from having any responsibility for the altercation. My feelings are, "Why bother?" Just accept responsibility for being part of the problem and start to resolve the issue.

Let me try an example. I have a sister three years older. Ever since I came into the world I think she has had a problem with my being around. Throughout our childhood and adolescence I was a source of irritation. We sort of moved through it as young adults, but the basic problem was still there. The details of the story are rather "juicy" but not that important to my point. Many years ago, my sister sued me because one of her ex-husbands convinced her that I was stealing from her. After $25,000 in legal expenses for her, she dropped the suit. She had no case. I knew that I had done nothing wrong to my sister. But I also knew that just my presence was part of the problem. I needed to assume that responsibility and attempt to resolve it. Eventually we did, but even though I was innocent of any charge, I was the problem. We have dealt with that and moved on with life. *Agape* works.

This brings up another issue, blame. Too many people spend too much time trying to figure out, "Who is to blame?" For the most part, unless it is a court of law, this exercise is a waste of time and never really proves who is right or wrong. Justice is not always served in courtrooms. Cases in point: OJ Simpson, Michael Jackson, Robert Blake and many other wealthy people.

When I was involved in a drug rehabilitation center as the program director, it was always interesting to watch the attitude of new patients. If their mantra was to blame everyone else for their drug problem, then I knew they would reap little benefit from the program. Each person must assume responsibility for his/her life and for what they have or have not done in it.

Forget blame. Move forward.

The ethics of Jesus demand that we forgive ourselves and others.

<u>STANDARD 4</u>: Each and every ethical/moral decision is different and needs to be made on the circumstances, not a law or rule.

This standard is probably the most difficult one to understand because we were not raised to think this way. Growing up I suspect your head was filled with the saying, "A rule is a rule." Rules are not to be broken, without paying a price. There are no exceptions. But this Standard is suggesting rules can and, at times, *must* be broken depending upon the situation.

In Judaism, on the day of the Sabbath from sunup to sundown, no work can be done. Religious leaders then went on to define "work" and what work might be acceptable on the Sabbath. On this particular day, Jesus was going through the fields with his disciples and they illegally plucked ears of grain because they were hungry. Some of the religious leaders saw it and said to him, "Look what your disciples are doing, which is not lawful on the Sabbath." Jesus responded, "Have you not read what David did when he was hungry, and those who were with him? They entered the house of God and they ate of the bread of the Presence, which was unlawful for him to eat nor for those who were with him, but only for the priests." The religious leaders did not answer and Jesus continues, "The Sabbath was made for man, not man for the Sabbath." (Mark 2:23-28)

In that situation Jesus did not care what the law said. His men were hungry and he felt they needed to eat regardless of the law. The Standard is saying just that: One must look at the circumstance (not the law) and then make a decision based on doing the most loving thing for the most people.

The following story is found in Joseph Fletcher's book, ***"Situation Ethics***." (Westminster Press, Philadelphia, 1966 pages 164-5). "As the Russians drove westward to meet the Americans and the British at the Elbe, a Soviet patrol picked up a Mrs. Bergmeier foraging food for her three children. Unable to even get word to her children, she was taken off to a prison camp in the Ukraine. Her husband had been captured in the battle of the Bulge and taken to a camp in Wales.

When he returned to Berlin, he spent weeks and weeks rounding up his children: two (Ilse, twelve, and Paul, ten) were found in a detention school run by the Russians and the oldest Hans, fifteen, was found hiding in a cellar near the Alexander Platz. Their mother's whereabouts remained a mystery, but they never stopped searching. She, more than anything else, was needed to reunitc the family in that dire situation of hunger, chaos and fear.

Meanwhile, in the Ukraine, Mrs. Bergmeier learned through a sympathetic commandant that her husband and children were trying to keep together and find her. But the rules allowed them to release her for only two reasons: (1) illness needing medical facilities beyond the camp's capabilities, in which case she would be sent to a soviet hospital elsewhere, and (2) pregnancy, in which case she would be returned to Germany as a liability.

She turned things over in her mind and finally asked a friendly Volga guard to impregnate her, which he did. Obviously, the woman was committing adultery which is not acceptable in almost all religions. This is a grave sin she was committing and to make matters worse, the newborn child would be labeled as a 'bastard.' Her act was not to be taken lightly as just sex, because she was "horny" in a prison camp.

Her condition being medically verified, she was sent back to Berlin and her family. They welcomed her with open arms, even when she told them how she had managed it. When the child was born they loved him more than all the rest, with the view that little Dietrich had done more for them than anyone else.

When it was time for him to be christened, they took him to the pastor on a Sunday afternoon. After the ceremony, they sent Dietrich home with their other children and sat down in the pastor's study, to ask him whether they were right to feel the way they did about Mrs. Bergmeier and Dietrich. Should they be grateful to the German Volga? Had Mrs. Bergmeier done a good and right thing?"

I know too many Christian churches that would condemn Mrs. Bergmeier as an adulteress and excommunicate her because she had gone against the rules of the church concerning adultery. They would probably urge Mr. Bergmeier to sue for divorce and would label little Dietrich a bastard. This is the legalism of some churches and is far removed from the ethics of Jesus. With his ethics as the foundation, one would take into account all extenuating circumstances. What Mrs. Bergmeier did was the right thing to bring this family back together. From the little we know about all the facts, there seemed to be no other alternative. It was adultery done in the name of *agape,* not lust. I suspect as she was having sex with the Volga guard she was guilt ridden, but it was the most loving thing she could do for her family and their future. Again, taking the ethics of Jesus into consideration, little Dietrich was legally a bastard, but in the eyes of the ethics of Jesus, he was a hero whose presence made all this happen.

This is what Standard 4 means when it states that every ethical/moral decision is to be made depending upon the circumstances of the situation. There are some, maybe even many, Christians who will have a difficult time with this. They are only comfortable living under the law, which is black and white and has no wiggle room.

I would like to share another story in which I am making three points. 1. I need to explain what I call a "Freedom Camp", a unique experience for participants to live in the Kingdom of *Agape.* 2. The reaction of some clergy to such a Kingdom. 3. How a teenager radically changed my theology. I can remember the incident vividly, as if it happened yesterday. I can visualize in my mind the place where this happened. It was that life changing. It was in 1963, in Hawai'i, and I was the youth minister to some 350 teenagers. Two or three times a year I would take the youth out to the north shore of Oahu for a weekend conference at our Episcopal church camp/conference center. My theme at this conference was called "Jesus Alive," a positive reaction to the "God is Dead" slogan. I called all my camps "Freedom Camps" because they were free from any rules. We would go to camp on Friday evening and after dinner I would gather the 100 to 125 youth and talk about our objectives for the weekend. One of the things I told them was that there would be *no* rules for the weekend, but we would live by the standard of The Great Commandment, which is to love self, neighbor, Creator. The youth loved this concept, but found it much more difficult to live with than they imagined. They found out that such a standard demanded that they had to make all kinds of decisions that they ordinarily would *not* have to make in other camps that had pages of rules to guide them. I would remind the young people that on Sunday afternoon before we left camp there would be a self-evaluation that consisted of asking themselves if they would be proud of their behavior during the weekend? Would their parents be proud of their actions? How about me, the rest of the staff, the Bishop and above all their Creator?

Many of the youth could not believe what they heard. A few thought it was license to go crazy and a few gave it their best try. However, those who had been to previous camps with me understood the concept, and did a fantastic job of helping the newcomers comprehend living in a Kingdom of Love. If a youth brought cigarettes or booze or drugs, the "old timers" would get rid of the contraband. They self-policed and we had next to no behavior problems at our camps. If there was an occasional incident, it was dealt with quickly, firmly and lovingly. This is how a Freedom Camp operatcs.

Some clergy (the legalists) thought that this approach would produce total bedlam and that the young people would run amuck. They felt the only way to control teenagers was with rules. This amazed me. The very people who should understand that the Kingdom is about love, not rules, were only comfortable living in the Kingdom of rules. Point two: Some clergy are much more comfortable with rules than a Kingdom of Love.

My volunteer staff, mostly college age students and young adults, really enjoyed these camps and I never had a problem recruiting them. They too enjoyed living for a fleeting moment in the Kingdom of Love and the weekend was not a total wipeout for them. They were able to get some sleep because, unbeknownst to the youth, the staff took four hour shifts of being "around" either hanging with the youth who wanted to stay up late, perhaps reading or maybe simply wandering around the camp. All staff had at least six hours of sleep a night so they could face Monday morning. However, some of the youth who did not have much sleep could not make it to school on Monday.

It was at one of these camps that I was forced to face an issue. It was after our Saturday evening session, about 9:15. I was standing by the door of one of the cabins when a young man, about 16, came up to me and said, "Bil, you've really confused me. This morning your main theme seemed to be that Jesus' message was about loving everyone, including ourselves. Then this evening when you were talking about Paul you started talking about some people who perhaps shouldn't be loved, like those who were divorced, or had not accepted Jesus as their Christ or were homosexuals. I guess my question is how can you preach about loving everyone in the morning, but by the evening you start giving us lists of those who shouldn't be totally loved, accepted or forgiven. This just doesn't sound right to me!" I probably tried to defend myself, but then he excused himself to go to the campfire. This question threw me for a loop.

After a restless night I knew that this teenager was correct. ***The kingdom of Jesus is open to all! There can be no exceptions!*** Let me share a sidelight to this story. After college, this young man went to seminary and today is a priest in the Episcopal church. He is gay and lives with his longtime partner. I shall be eternally grateful to this person who not only set me straight that evening, but who also challenged me to make some radical changes in my thinking and my faith. This change came about because I finally heard what Jesus was saying: Everyone is welcomed into the Kingdom and there can never be any exceptions.

I do realize that it is not possible for a society to simply live by the guidelines of The Great Commandment. An orderly society needs laws and rules because most people feel more comfortable living within a known given; i.e., a rule or law. It would be utopian to think that a large group of people could successfully live under the umbrella of the ethics of Jesus. In such a utopia one would not need laws and rules. People would know that they are not to drive through a school zone at 60 mph while children were present. A sign simply needs to say "School Zone" and the driver would automatically slow to about 20 to 25 mph. Unfortunately, that is not the real world. Thus, we then need to post a speed limit and be prepared to enforce it. I believe most of the world wants to live under the law. It makes life black and white and seemingly simpler. But however easy it might seem to live this way, it very seldom has any wiggle room. I have found that *every* situation is unique and there can be no law that covers each and every circumstance. Some situations seem to be very similar, but when one looks closely at all the details there is a difference. Let us look at an example.

The law says one cannot murder without paying a price regardless of the circumstances. Then we meet a woman who had been abused by her partner for years, but was too frightened to leave. The man came home one evening drunk (as he did on many nights) and very angry. He started to physically abuse her one more time. She could take it no more. She was at the point where she thought, "I must kill him or maybe he will kill me or maim me for life." She killed him and went on trial for murder. Had we told a story about a man who, just one time, came home and physically abused his wife and she killed him, then that would be a very different story with a different response.

What is interesting to me in the first story is that it is not the police department who went on trial even though they had told her repeatedly that until her husband/ boyfriend did noticeable physical damage to her they could not help her. In my eyes, the police, who are supposedly there to protect, have failed and also need to be on trial. Then there is the judge or the legal system that is so complex and expensive that it is difficult for the average person to obtain the injunction(s) they need to keep the abusers away, far away. Why are not the judge and/or the courts on trial? They also failed to protect her. Then there is the abuser. Although he is dead, he needs to go on trial in absentia, because he is the villain in this story. There could also be other folks out there like a social worker who turned her or his back on the situation, or a neighbor who refused to call the police, or family members who turned the other way. Why don't they have to go to trial? No, it is only the woman who will be punished and sent to prison even though it was the system that failed her. The legal system does not necessarily mete out justice.

The ethics of Jesus demand that we look at every situation and all the details and then make decisions based on love. To say that the above-mentioned woman is a murderer is true. But, with the ethics of Jesus, if one were to examine every detail of her situation and make a judgment according to the circumstances, maybe the woman would be hailed as a hero who dealt with an evil person the only way society would allow her. Since the system would not support her in her quest to be rid of this abusive man, maybe she really did society a favor by eliminating him. What do you think?

With the ethics of Jesus one must evaluate every situation separately. One cannot make decisions based on the law of the land, the judicial system, canon law, the unwritten rules of the institution or family, one's conscience, past experiences, friendly advice from clergy, family or friends. Very seldom will you find that any of the above decisions were based on the law of love. As a result, I can give you examples that demonstrate that sometimes the most loving thing one could do is illegal or what some categorize as immoral. But each decision must be based on the ethics of Jesus, and if the decision goes against the law of the land then one must pay the price. The next chapter will give you some examples.

If one lives by the ethics of Jesus one must be prepared to "swim against the current," realizing that society does *not* appreciate someone who fights the system. (Ask Jesus!)

I have been in trouble during my entire ministry because I have fought the system. When I was first ordained, I secretly officiated at the marriages of people who had been divorced because the church had antiquated rules against the remarrying of divorced people. They still have unloving rules and refuse to marry people who have been married multiple times. Over the years I have seen that some folks are "slow learners" when it comes to choosing the right partner. By the third or fourth marriage not only do they make better choices, but they also work harder and better at keeping the marriage going. As an agent of Christianity and a follower of a man who talked about forgiving "70 x 7" times, I have no qualms about remarrying people if they think they have it right this time.

Until my dying days I shall oppose the institutional church and their rejection of people with alternative lifestyles. The ethics of Jesus tell me over and over that there must be the full acceptance of everyone. I have a real problem when the church starts making lists of those who are not totally accepted (and I mean *totally*). As soon as the church develops a list of those not accepted and forgiven then we have a new church or cult based on some obscure passages in the Bible or their own prejudices. People with alternative life styles *must* have full rights in the church, which includes the blessing of gay/lesbian relationships. (We cannot marry them because of antiquated civil laws based on ignorance.)

I want to see more gay and lesbian clergy come out of the closet, be honest with themselves, stop living the lie and be able to serve the church in every capacity - even to be elected bishops. I want to be an instrument to help gay and lesbian clergy and laity live life to the fullest. This means forcing the institution to recognize its unloving and unaccepting position.

I think infant baptism is wrong. I have been outspoken about it. The early church did not baptize children, because that would make them eligible to be fed to the lions. It was a custom promoted by the church in the fourth century when it decided that all non-baptized people, including children, would go to hell if they were not baptized. Since there is no such place called "hell" and since entering the Kingdom of Love is not dependent on a "washing," infant baptism is no longer important.

I do believe that the church should have some sort of ceremony welcoming an infant into that particular denomination. But allow the child to grow up and make that decision for him or herself as to whether Jesus is going to be their Christ or not. (I have recently read where someone considered infant baptism a form of child abuse…an interesting thought.) Christian freedom is about allowing people to make choices. Unfortunately, too many parents use baptism as a sort of Christian lucky rabbit's foot. The idea of their child going to hell is still in the back of their mind, so, to be on the safe side, they want baptism - the rabbit's foot. Over the years, I have found some of these same parents do not darken the doors of the church except for baptisms, weddings and funerals. They have no intention of raising their child in a Christian community. Why not allow the child to grow up and make that decision when they are able to follow through with the commitment?

This stance of mine concerning infant baptism is not a popular one in the institutional church. I think it must have something to do with economics. If we don't baptize their child then maybe the parents or grandparents or both would leave the church. Perhaps, while preparing families for baptism the clergy need to explain to young families that there is no such place as hell and their child can enter into the Kingdom of Love any time. (Because I am a believer in the ethics of Jesus, I think it is unloving *not* to baptize a child whose parents, involved in the church, think it is important. Perhaps the most loving thing to do is to baptize the infant and remind the parents that nothing is going to happen to that child unless they lead the way and show the child how important it is to have a relationship with a Higher Power.)

There are more, many more issues against which I rally. But the point I am making is that to live by the law of love is not easy, but it is the right thing to do if one subscribes to the ethics of Jesus.

THE HOW TO...

How then does one make decisions based on the ethics of Jesus? It is really rather easy. When one makes ethical decisions they are based on seven underlying questions. **What? Why? Who? When? Where? Which? How?** With the ethics of Jesus the answers are relatively simple.

The **what** is love.

The **why** is because we are made in the image of love and our principle task is to do just that.

The **who** is self, neighbor, Creator/Creation.

The **when** is now.

The **where** is here and every place we are.

The **which** is the most loving thing one can do for the most people.

The **how** includes acceptance, forgiveness and reading about how Jesus did life.

The **how** also includes understanding the concept of *agape*. It is suspicious of one's conscience and makes decisions based on the details of every given situation that can bump headlong into the law of the land.

I like the idea expressed in Joseph Fletcher's book, ***Situation Ethics*** (Westminster Press, Philadelphia 1966): "Justice is Christian love using its head, calculating its duties, obligations, opportunities, resources" (page 95). *Agape* cannot simply refer to a law to justify one's position. One must think through "using its head" in each situation because every situation is different. *Agape* must make calculations.

Let us look at a physician in an emergency room who must decide to whom to give the hospital's last unit of plasma. Will it be to a young mother with three children, a skid row drug addict or an older wealthy man who was driving drunk and ran into a bridge? The doctor could be sentimentalized into thinking that he needs to be impartial and simply flip a coin to make his choice. But that is not reality. *Agape* must calculate the situation. The doctor must make estimates about serving the many rather than the few. *Agape* is preferential. It does make estimates. It is justice distributed. The plasma goes to the young mother.

We now have the tools to do the ethics of Jesus. Let's try to use them with the situations given in the next chapter.

"If anyone wants to become my follower, let them deny themselves and take up their cross and follow me. For those who want to save their life (*by not loving, accepting, forgiving*) will lose it and those who lose their life (*by loving, accepting, forgiving*) for my sake will find it." (Matthew 16:24, 25)

CHAPTER 8

WHAT WOULD YOU DO?

Most of the time I enjoy reading the comic strip "Pearls Before Swine." (Sometimes it struggles too much to be funny and then it's not.) The title always reminds me of my parents. My mother's name was Pearl. My dad's middle name was Hamilton and people called him Ham. My dad told me the epitaph they wanted on their gravestones was "Pearls Thrown Before Swine." Anyway, in this comic strip the pig is asking the mouse, "What are you writing?" Mouse: "I'm trying to come up with my own personal motto…something I can live by." Pig: "Oh, I have a few…'love yourself'…'Laugh and the world laughs with you'…'Today is the first day of the rest of your life'…What did you write?" Mouse replies, "Crush the little people…I'm trying to be realistic!"

I am going to share some stories in which people have had to make ethical decisions about themselves and others. The story will be told up to the conclusion. Then I want you to finish the story (in your mind) relating what you would have done using the ethics of Jesus. ("Crush the little people" should not be a choice.) At that point, I shall then share how the story ended and relate how the ethics of Jesus apply.

There are limitations to this process in that I can only give you some of the story; otherwise it could require volumes to give you all the details.

To assist in the process let us quickly review the last chapter.

REMINDERS:

1. **A*gape* love is not about liking.**
2. **Tough love is about love.**
3. **Beware of your prejudices.**
4. **The opposite of love is not hate. (It's indifference.)**
5. **Beware of your conscience. It should NOT be your guide.**
6. **Love and justice are the same because justice (moral) is love distributed.**

STANDARDS:

1. ***Agape* love is the foundation of the ethics of Jesus; only one thing is right and good, *agape.***
2. ***Agape* must include acceptance of ourselves and every other human being, whether we like them or not.**
3. ***Agape* demands that we forgive self and others immediately.**
4. **Each and every ethical/moral decision is different and needs to be made depending on the circumstances, not a rule or law.**

The What? Why? Who? When? Where? Which? How? Questions are all answered by "love of self, neighbor, Creator/Creation" centered on immediate forgiveness and acceptance. Remember, the *agape* is for the most number of people involved.

STORY 1

Linda came to counseling because she felt her marriage was in a great deal of trouble. Her husband refused to come with her because he said she was the problem and if she fixed the problem the marriage would be fine. They had two small children, ages three and a half and five. Her husband, Fred, worked out of the house and she had a full time job which brought in most of their income. Fred was involved in a religion, really a cult, which advocated the husband as the absolute head of the house, the wife as subservient and totally obedient children. Linda did not buy into this thinking and which was the source for many of their problems.

After a few sessions with Linda trying to sort out all the issues, I asked her to ask her husband if he would come in either alone or with her so that I could hear his side of the story.

He agreed and came in with her. He spoke about her fiery temper, her violent outbursts, her abusive (she was a yeller) handling of the children. Fred said there would be no problems if she would join his church, do what they say and assume her wifely position. There were other issues he brought up, but the underlying one was that he was very controlling. I suggested that they both come into counseling and that we try to arrive at some compromising behavior. He refused on the grounds that his religion spelled out very clearly what Scripture advocated and that counseling would do no good. It was obvious Fred was not going to give up control.

Linda came back for a few more sessions primarily to figure out what she was going to do. I suggested she really had limited choices. She could do as he said, live with the marriage the way it was, or go for a separation. Linda admitted that she did not love Fred in a romantic way any more and she then asked me which choice I saw as her best option?

What would you have told Linda?

What happened:

I told her that I did not see much hope for the marriage, but I gave her a plan.

She should obtain a legal separation, which would allow both parties and the children to have a respite from the constant bickering. It would also allow each person to see what it is like to live alone, shuffling the two small children back and forth, suffering financial hardships and dealing with lots of loneliness. This approach either brings people back together willing to make compromises or allows them to realize that the marriage is finished and they need to see a divorce attorney. I did not see Linda again and had no idea what she did.

Fifteen years later I saw Linda at a church we were attending. She introduced herself to me and told me that she had been in counseling with me. Then she said, "I wish I had taken your advice then, but I waited seven years before I did anything. By that time the children and I were totally messed up and we're still picking up the pieces!"

Marriage is a great institution if it is done correctly and two people are willing to work on it. There are always issues in a marriage, but if people are willing to compromise and resolve the issues then, there are no long-term problems. However, if people ignore the issues and don't resolve them then the marriage is doomed for failure and it is best that they divorce so that everyone can have a new beginning, a figurative Easter. Linda could have saved herself and her children a great deal of grief if she had opted for the separation. It would have been the most loving thing to do for everyone involved.

STORY 2

He was in his late seventies and in the final stages of Alzheimer's. He recognized no one - his wife of 50 plus years, his children or any of the staff who cared for his daily needs. Most of the day he simply sat and stared into space or fell asleep. He had been a very successful doctor, but also had had many affairs with his nursing staff and patients. His faithful wife had no choice but to tolerate his bad behavior and keep such information from their four children. The children were grown and lived away from the area. Only occasionally would they come to see their father who had no idea who they were. His wife came to the care facility on a daily basis, helped to feed and clothe her husband and then sat with him reading and knitting.

One day the wife started talking with a gentleman who also came on a daily basis to visit his wife, who was at the same stage with her Alzheimer's - she recognized no one and was just barely living. They started talking and sharing. They ate lunch together every day at the care home. Then one evening they went to the movies together. They held each other's hand and talked about their loneliness. Neither of them had anyone with whom they could share their true feelings. They kissed and started heavy "petting." They felt, at a certain level, they were in love and wanted to go further. Both of them were committed Christians who felt guilty about their actions. The wife came to me, shared her story and asked, "What do you think I should do?" We dialogued. She told me about some of her husband's affairs and how he would flaunt them in her face asking, "And what are you going to do about it? I'll take the children, throw you out and leave you with nothing!" Back in those days there was not much a woman could do about being in an abusive situation. He had all the cards. He was emotionally abusive to her and had even hit her. At one point, she hated him but knew she had to live with it. After he was diagnosed, he left his medical practice and hung around the house becoming progressively worse. She then placed him in a facility for Alzheimer patients.

At this time in the story, he was for all intents and purposes "dead," as was the wife of my client's male friend. It was only medications and excellent expensive care that were keeping their spouses' alive.

They both knew that if their children ever found out about the two of them getting together they would be livid.

If you were in my place, what would you tell the woman? Don't have an affair with the other man because that would be adultery? Or would you remind her that Jesus had suggested if you even look at a woman lustfully..." (Matthew 5:228) you have already committed adultery, with your eyes and mind. (The scholars of the Jesus Seminar don't think Jesus ever said this. It is very much out of character.)

Would you tell her that if it weren't for medication, excellent care and medical insurance, both the husband and wife would be dead and this wouldn't be an issue. The lives of the two spouses with advanced stages of Alzheimer's seemingly had no purpose. Or would you tell them to have the affair, be discreet and don't tell the children or anyone else. It was really no one's business, but simply between the two of them.

Perhaps you could suggest still another alternative. What would you tell this woman to do?

What did I tell her to do? Nothing! My role was to gather information for her sake and mine. She needed to hear herself. She needed to deal with all the anger she had at her husband for years of emotional and some physical abuse. She had to hear herself and her feelings about the fact that her children were only supporting her superficially. I needed to ask hard questions, be non-judgmental and to listen carefully to what she was telling me. Together we explored every possible alternative and discussed them thoroughly. I wanted *her* to think through this situation.

When it was obvious we were finished, she asked me, "Bil, what would you do?" I replied, "I can't tell you because I am not in your situation and your circumstances are unique to you. You are a lifelong Christian, a mature woman who has led an exemplary life under difficult circumstances. You need to weigh all the information we discussed and make your decision. It's your life and only you are responsible for it. I do *not* believe that there will be a judgment from above for whatever action you choose. The important thing is that you have thought a great deal about it before you decided.

Whatever your decision, I respect who you are and would never make a judgment. My role as a fellow Christian is to accept you and love you." I doubt that this was the answer she wanted from me, but maybe it was.

What did she do? I have no idea! I do know that when I saw her in church she had a glow about her that, whatever she did, made her life better.

I use this example to emphasize these ideas: Every decision is unique. There is ***NO*** universal answer to a specific situation. Each one is different. It is not our role to judge, but simply to accept, forgive and love. I find this approach makes my life a great deal simpler. I don't have to judge, condemn and reject people whose situation I really do not totally understand.

STORY 3

Mike went to work as a project manager for a large manufacturing company in 1989. Within two years he had brought in so much business the company promoted him to Vice President overseeing sales for the entire division. He worked closely with a co-leader and they were able to bring a marginal group in their division to be the third largest in the entire company with annual revenues in the hundreds of millions. When Mike's co-leader retired in a few years, he was replaced by an authoritarian man, Ray, who micro-managed everyone through bullying and intimidation. He seemed to have the propensity to alienate one and all, resulting in many managers and staff transferring to other divisions. The morale was terrible and this division gained the reputation for being a difficult and undesirable place to work. Sales declined. The contracts developed problems and Ray's only method of dealing with these issues was to harass and denigrate people. Mike found it difficult to work with this man He deplored the way Ray spoke to Mike's staff. Mike tried to talk with Ray but it was impossible because he let Mike know it was Ray's way or no way. Mike spoke with higher management, but no one wanted to listen. Mike had to make a choice. 1. Stay where he was and tolerate the way Ray treated people and micro-managed everyone. 2. Leave the corporation and try to find a new job in a different field in a down market even though this could be a black mark on his resume. 3. Transfer to another division, take a pay cut and demotion. With the ethics of Jesus in mind, what would you do?

What actually happened:

Mike, a committed Christian, could not tolerate the way Ray treated people as things/objects. Since no one in upper management would listen, Mike knew things were not going to change. Mike also knew that jobs were scarce and that he had a family to look after and financial obligations to fulfill. Going out job-hunting in a depressed market would not be a responsible loving thing to do. His best and most loving action was to transfer, taking the demotion and cut in pay while being responsible to his family and obligations. This is *agape* in action.

PS. Three years after Mike left Ray's division, the company fired Ray.

STORY 4

Don had been diagnosed with multiple sclerosis at the age of fifty. In the following fifteen years he led a very full life. He and his wife traveled all over the USA, in an RV, visiting family and friends and seeing the country. The two of them were heavily involved in all sorts of activities. Little by little Don deteriorated. First, a cane and then crutches. Next came a wheelchair. Then they bought an electric one. They purchased a van specially fitted with a ramp and made their RV wheelchair accessible. They continued traveling but then it came to a point where Don could no longer drive. He supervised but his wife had to do all the driving, setting up at RV camps, filling and emptying tanks, cooking and a myriad of other duties. As much as Don enjoyed the traveling, his wife found it exhausting. The travel had to stop. Don was losing feelings in his legs, arms and hands. His brain was still sharp, but now he needed to be waited on full time. The pain was constant. He could not sleep in a bed so he lived in his wheelchair. He knew the end was coming. He talked with a friend and told him that he was thinking about ending his life. He knew the final steps of MS would be de-humanizing. He did not want to go through it or drag his family through the agony. He had saved hundreds of pills for a few years and felt that now he had to make the final preparations to end his life. Although his wife did not want him to die, she did not want him to suffer the indignities of a lingering MS death. He had spoken with each of his adult children. Again, they did not want their dad to die, but they also did not want to see him suffer anymore. He had spoken with his sister who agreed that his life offered little or no quality. Finally, he confided to a close friend that he wanted to end his life. He knew his friend had helped others. Would he help him?

How would you respond to Don? What would be the most loving thing you could do to support him?

What happened: Let me start by saying that I feel that every human being is responsible for her or himself. As Paul says, "...work out your own salvation with fear and trembling." (Philippians 2:12) We are responsible for no one else's life but our own. Jesus said nothing about the government or religious groups working out my life or yours. Don had to do what he felt was best for him. He and his friend talked long and hard about his decision. He had crossed every "t" and dotted every "i." This is what he wanted to do and his immediate family concurred. He decided on the time and place. His friend ground his pills and made certain that he was able to ingest them. When all the pills were gone, his friend left and Don's wife stayed with him as he died. He was dead within a few days. In this story, I feel Don did what was the most loving thing for the most people. His family was happy that he did not have to suffer any more. They had all said goodbye to him and were feeling that they had all done what he wanted. The funeral home chapel was packed with people who wanted to celebrate the life of a fellow human being who had lived his life fully and knew that he needed to pull the plug and die in peace.

What about the friend who helped Don die? Legally he could be charged with assisting Don's committing suicide. Did he do a kind and loving thing?

STORY 5

Sam and Karen, an older couple, wanted to be married in the church they attended. She had never been married; Sam had been married three times before, but had been single for twenty years. They approached the Rector of the parish and asked him if he would officiate at a very small wedding, preferably in the church. When the Rector heard that Sam had been married three times, he told them that Sam must apply to the Diocese and receive permission from the bishop. Sam needed to send to the bishop all the details of each of the three marriages, as well as the three divorce decrees. The last marriage had been twenty years ago and Sam could hardly remember the details. The Rector also shared with him that once he had done all that work, he still might not receive permission. Sam and Karen did not want to go through all that past negative history, so they came to me and asked me to marry them in their home with only his son and his wife in attendance. I knew that if I refused the couple they would have left the church perceiving it as judgmental and non-accepting. I also realized that if I did officiate and marry them without seeking permission from the bishop and diocese, I would be in violation of my ordination vows and could get into a great deal of trouble with both the bishop and the diocese.

What would you do if you were me? Refuse the couple or marry them?

What happened:

Common sense and love won out in this instance. I married the couple in their home with only his son and his wife in attendance. My rationale: I hope the world does not keep rubbing my nose in a mistake(s) I made twenty years ago as the church wanted to do to Sam. The church needs to be a loving, forgiving, accepting community that allows people to accept their past as just that, their past. The institutional church keeps claiming it believes in new beginnings (Good Friday and Easter), but in this instance I do not see or feel love and acceptance. Rather, I see the church as a legalistic, unloving, unforgiving and unaccepting community. Throughout my entire ministry I have fought the church's unforgiving stance concerning divorce and have married many couples who did not want to regurgitate their past in order to be married in a church. Sam and Karen were involved in the church. They attended on Sundays, pledged and participated in parish activities. The church was willing to allow them to do all that, but then when the couple wanted to be married, the church became legalistic and judgmental. This is not the spirit of *agape*. In counseling with Sam and Karen I believed that they were in love, had dealt creatively with the past and were going to work diligently to make this marriage work.

What about my ordination vows in which I stated publicly that I would "obey your bishop and other ministers who may have authority over you and your work?" (***Book of Common Prayer,*** "Ordination: Deacon", page 538.) My first allegiance is to Jesus, my Christ, who, in my eyes, fought his religious institution until his crucifixion. In my many years of being ordained an Episcopal priest, I have seen the institution wrong on many issues. I have rallied against its discrimination toward women, gays, lesbians and those with alternative lifestyles, the homeless, the poor, the divorced and the building of edifices in lieu of ministering to and loving our fellow human beings. To be defrocked for loving people and calling attention to the church's hypocrisy would be a badge of honor.

STORY 6

Mary was a long time friend of our family. She had been a member of one of my parishes and became like family to us. About a dozen years ago she left the Episcopal Church and became involved in an evangelical sect. They taught her to be homophobic. She seemed to be very happy being involved with this narrow, limited sort of thinking so I chose not to challenge her about this issue. Shortly after the Rt. Rev. Gene Robinson (an openly gay Episcopal priest who was living with his long-time partner) was consecrated bishop of New Hampshire, she came to visit us and suggested the consecration of Gene Robinson was against the law of God. That pushed my button and I challenged her homophobic thinking. She claimed she had many friends who were gay which made it even worse. Why would one be friends with anyone who was against who you were/are? For a short period of time, she and I communicated about this issue via email, but it became obvious that this was a stalemate. She did not care about any facts having to do with why people are gay. In her eyes, homosexuality was a sin and gay men needed to choose heterosexuality. Case closed.

I am most uncomfortable with homophobics and see them as diametrically opposed to the spirit of agape. I also do not want to host anyone in our home who is blatantly homophobic, racist, chauvinistic or bigoted.

How do you feel about my stance? Would you try to convince me otherwise? If so, how? Would you invite this person into your home as a guest?

What happened:

Mary has not tried to come to visit us since our discussions. Once she tried to arrange a visit, but we were not available. For many years I have been very straightforward in letting people in our home know that pejorative words about other races or religions, ethnic jokes, racist or sexist jokes would not be welcomed. One time, I had to ask a woman to leave our house because she would not stop telling racist jokes and using the "n" word. She was stunned when she left and we have never seen her again. It was at that time I developed the stance that in the name of *agape*, I shall always challenge intolerance. I have been questioned about this stance ("You are just like them."), but feel that as a follower of a man who preached an accepting, forgiving *agape* love I need to stand up to people who openly show their intolerance. I have developed, derived from the teachings and actions of Jesus, the idea that any form of intolerance has to be questioned by believers or *agape* will never happen. I still love our friend Mary, but I do not like who she has become: a rather narrow-minded and bigoted individual.

How do your feel about a follower of Jesus challenging intolerance?

STORY 7

A staff doctor asked the chaplain to drop in on Jim. In his middle forties, married, five children, Jim had been in the hospital for over a month, having a series of biopsies, X-rays, MRIs, blood tests, even exploratory surgery, to diagnose a breakdown in his digestive system.

The chaplain went to Jim's room. Jim explained he would have cramps after each meal. He tried the "Tums" route and every sort of over-the-counter digestive aid there was, all to no avail. One doctor thought it might be an ulcer, but Jim was too busy at being a construction engineer to take the time to have the necessary tests. The two were just getting into things when the nurse arrived to ready him for more tests. The chaplain said he would return tomorrow to see what the results were.

The next afternoon the chaplain found Jim in the solarium looking very downcast. The chaplain asked him about the test results. Jim responded, "They tell me I have about a maximum of three years left, unless a cure is found in that time. They can give me medicines to keep me alive, but eventually my illness will kill me. Each pill costs $140 and it lasts 3 days. If I stop taking them, I have about six months left. To make matters worse, my company has my life insured for $250,000 double indemnity. That's all the insurance or assets (except our house with a mortgage) I have to leave to my wife and children. If I live past next

October, then the policy, when it comes up for renewal, will be cancelled.

"If I don't take the pills and die, my family will have some security. If I'm still alive after October, they will have nothing when I die except huge unpaid medical bills, which will take our home and leave my family in the poor house. With the double indemnity on the insurance they would then have $500,000 and they could carry on reasonably well.

"To me the only viable option is to stop taking the pills and make certain that I die before the insurance policy is cancelled. Pastor, how does it look to you? What would you do? I want to do the right thing."

What would you do if you were Jim? If you were the chaplain what would you tell Jim to do?

What happened?

I really don't know what Jim did because I borrowed this illustration from Joseph Fletcher's book**, *"Situation Ethics*"** (pages 165-66).

What would I tell Jim? I would validate his decision to stop taking the pills and to leave his family with something. There was nothing that was going to make it possible for him to live. Death within two to six months was a given. As difficult as it was going to be to tell his wife, their parents, his children, his close friends his wish, it could be framed in such a way as to indicate to them that he wanted to make it the best two, three months in all their lives. He wanted them to celebrate his life and not be focused on his death. He would remind them that every human life is terminal. We have no guarantee that any of us shall be here to greet the new day. The next period of time was to be spent in doing a special family event and that every day was to be lived to its fullest. He would have his chance to say his goodbyes and to make certain that everything was in order so that his family could move on as easily as possible. Finally, he would remind them that this is *agape*...doing the very best he could for the greatest number of people.

STORY 8

I had known Sarah since she was 20. She had come to me for some pastoral counseling and we remained friends. I officiated at her marriage to Michael. A few years later their first child was born prematurely and lived for seven hours. A couple of years later their second child was born at twenty-four weeks in the pregnancy. I hurried to the hospital and held this baby in the palm of one hand as I baptized her. We did not expect her to live, but she was a fighter. She, Emma, had thirteen operations on her brain in her first year of life, which caused a great deal of damage. In the second year she had three more operations. The baby's brain was badly injured from all those operations and the future looked bleak, but her Mom and Dad took excellent care of her and gave her every conceivable opportunity. It was obvious Emma would never walk, talk, and be able to play like other children or do much more than smile.

Sarah had to become a full time caregiver, which after a few years took a toll on their marriage. They went to the state and asked for financial assistance to bring in supplemental help, but were told that the only way they could receive any aid was to put Emma in a foster home They would not fund the parents directly for in home help. Sarah and Michael could not believe it, but much against their will, they put Emma in a foster home. They visited every day and took care of Emma's needs, but it was not the same as being at home. Emma started to fail. Then her shunt malfunctioned and she was hospitalized. The doctors said she must have another brain operation and a new shunt or she would die. They called me and asked what they should do. They did not want to put Emma through this because it would mean more brain damage and lessen even more her already limited ability to function. If they left Emma in the hospital they would perform heroics and Emma would be kept alive only by machines.

With *agape* in mind what would you tell Sarah and Michael?

What happened:

First, we discussed leaving Emma in the hospital. A religious group administered it and it was obvious they would do heroics to Emma and would not abide by the wishes of the parents. The first decision was to get Emma out of that hospital as quickly as possible so that the parents could be in charge.

Once they had Emma back in their home we then discussed her future. She would never be better and with another operation on her brain she could lose even more of her very limited capabilities. By not replacing the shunt she would certainly die and the projected date was during the Christmas holidays. The parents had already discussed this possibility and had decided no more operations on Emma. Reluctantly, they were willing to allow her to die knowing that this would be the most loving thing for everyone. Emma had led life to her fullest and now must be allowed to move on. It was a very emotional decision with everyone on both sides of the family shedding lots of tears. Some questioned the decision but the parents stood firm. I supported them to the hilt. Emma had done a great job of sensitizing the world around her. Everyone loved her in spite of all her challenges. Let her go.

Emma died Christmas night, a very sad time to die, but the parents knew that they had made an *agape* decision. What would you have done?

STORY 9

Tony was a world-renowned evangelical preacher. He had been invited to come to Hawai'i and preach. Coming from the east coast, his body's time clock was way off and in the middle of the night he was wide awake and ready to go to work. It was 3AM when Tony decided to get up and find a coffee shop. Not too far from his hotel he found an open diner and went in to order a cup of coffee. It was a busy place, even at that hour of the morning. After he ordered his cup of coffee Tony noticed that there was a group of women seated not far from him. It became obvious that they were "women of the night" who had just finished work. Tony was fascinated. The women were just sitting around chatting about business, their dreams and frustrations just as if their lives were no different from anyone else's. Tony could not help but eavesdrop. One woman stated that she was having a birthday tomorrow and that she had never had a birthday party. Her parents had been totally dysfunctional and she was raised on the streets. Tony had an idea. He would arrange a birthday party for her.

About dawn the women had all left and Tony went up to the manager and asked if the women came here often. The manager told him that they came every night between 3 and 4 a.m. and left about dawn. Tony asked if it would be possible to arrange a birthday party for one of the women. The manager said, "Of course. Who's going to pay?" Tony said he would cover all expenses. Then he and the manager discussed details.

Did Tony do a good thing? After all, in the eyes of society and the police, these women were practicing something illegal and immoral. Should Tony have minded his own business and not participated in an activity, which could possibly be construed as condoning the lifestyle of these women?

What happened:

The surprise party happened. The next night/early morning the women were all gathered as usual. The early arrivals were clued in as to why there were decorations in the restaurant but kept it a secret. The birthday woman arrived and shortly thereafter a cake with lighted candles, flowers and some gifts were brought to the table. Everyone started to sing "Happy Birthday" and the birthday lady broke down in tears. When she had gathered her wits, she wanted to know who had done this? The manager pointed to Tony in the corner. He came over, introduced himself, sat down with them and enjoyed some cake. The woman came over, with tears streaming down her face, and gave Tony a hug and a kiss on the cheek. She told him it was the nicest thing anyone had ever done for her.

My reaction: This action of Tony's was *agape* at its best. Tony crossed all sorts of barriers to honor and recognize another human being who was a victim of the ills of society. He gave her dignity and by accepting her as she was he gave her new life, perhaps only for a minute. This is something I see Jesus doing over and over, giving people new life. This is what we as followers are to do, accept and love, not judge and reject.

STORY 10

Maria was 33 years old, married to Greg who loved sports. They were his life. They had two daughters, 6 and 8 years old. Maria was also a sports fan who enjoyed sporting events with her husband. Very unexpectedly Maria found herself pregnant. She was afraid to tell Greg because he had made it very clear that parenting was not his thing and two children were all he wanted. Maria had very strong feelings against having an abortion and was feeling caught. She finally shared "the good news" with Greg. He was adamant. An abortion was in order. Maria could not do it. Greg then started going to sporting events with his buddies leaving Maria at home with the girls. He was very angry with her, which caused a great deal of tension in the house. Maria decided to continue with the pregnancy hoping that once Greg saw the baby he would change his mind.

When Maria was in her sixth month, Greg came home from work and announced that he had been to see an attorney that day and was moving ahead with a divorce. He told Maria that her choice of moving ahead with the child, against his strong feelings of not wanting another, indicated to him that Maria thought their marriage was not very important. He wanted out. Maria was devastated and came for advice. What would you tell her?

What happened:

Maria had the baby, a healthy 8½ pound boy. Greg had finalized the divorce and refused to see the baby or have anything to do with Maria. He felt this baby was responsible for destroying his otherwise good marriage.

I would have told Maria early in her pregnancy that she either had to reconsider her stance concerning abortion or risk losing her husband and maybe even the father of their children. I felt Maria gave Greg no choice when she knew very well his stance about having more children. I believe Maria was wrong to sacrifice her marriage, her children, her newborn and her future for the sake of a fetus which had the potential for life, but was not even close to be able to sustain life by itself. I would have reminded Maria that *agape* does the most loving thing for the greatest number of people which in this case might involve dozens of family members and friends who would be impacted by a divorce.

For me, the issue of abortion is a non-issue. The ethics of Jesus reinforces the idea that every human being is ultimately responsible for him or herself. Some try to make God, their parents or some tragedy in their past responsible, but that does not work when dealing with the realities of life. There can be no abortion law that covers every individual in each specific instance. I think abortion is only an issue because the fundamentalists and the Roman Catholics keep making it so. It seems, with both groups, facts and logic make no difference.

I do have a difficult time when individuals or religious groups set themselves up as the moral compass in our society. Obviously, their own biased thinking clouds the issue(s) and inevitably it seems to be their way or no way. Some other interesting thinking arises with their stance on abortion, such as:

1. Most fundamentalists and many Roman Catholics are against abortion, but *for* the death penalty. They seem to be for life in one instance and against it in another. This is rather inconsistent to me.

2. Inevitably, it seems to be *men* who keep wanting to make the decisions about what women are to do with their

lives and bodies. Too many men still see women as property and incapable of making their own decisions.

3. I cannot see where a life starts at conception. It is a fetus, not a child. A fetus cannot support itself in the early stages. I do not see either fundamentalists or Roman Catholics having funeral services for miscarriages. If they were consistent, then they should insist that every miscarriage be given a full funeral service.

4. Laws against abortion in no way stop abortions. If a woman wants an abortion she can have one, either with a doctor, a pill or a coat hanger.

With just these few examples, I hope the reader can start to see how the ethics of Jesus work in the everyday world. So different is this approach to life and daily living that many might be tempted to say, "It sounds much too difficult to make such drastic changes as the ethics of Jesus would demand. I think I'll just stay with the way I've been making decisions and allow the government, the church or my spouse to decide for me." I understand. The ethics of Jesus are not easy. But the rewards of living one's life using his ethics are rich. Please read the next chapter and then make up your mind.

"So faith, hope, love abide, these three; but the greatest of these is love." (1 Corinthians 13:13)

CHAPTER 9

THE CHALLENGES AHEAD

A car was moving slowly down a city street in a 35 mph speed zone. A policeman clocked it at 22 mph. He felt that the car was a traffic hazard so he turned on his siren and pulled the car over. There were five LOLs ("Little Old Ladies") in the vehicle. The driver was very attentive, but the 4 passengers were looking like zombies staring straight ahead, oblivious to the policeman pulling them over. He asked the driver if she knew why he stopped her?

Her reply was, "Because you can't catch anyone else?"

He said, "No, it's because you are driving 22 in a 35 mph zone and that's too slow. You could cause an accident!"

The LOL replied, "But officer, the sign says 22."

"Yes ma'am, but that is the number of this route, not the speed limit. I'm going to let you go but please observe the speed limit!"

"Yes, sir!" the LOL replied.

"But before you go I have a question. What is wrong with your four passengers? They're just staring ahead and haven't even moved during our conversation."

"I have no idea," said the LOL, "but we just came off 119!"

I have presented a great deal of material, rather quickly, perhaps much of it new to you and maybe a little difficult to digest. At this point, you might be feeling a little like you too "just got off the 119." This has been a quick trip through 2,000 years of Christianity in which I am suggesting that the institutional church has missed the essence of Jesus' message. For example:

- We have been told that Jesus was the Son of God and divine. We should have been hearing that Jesus was a charismatic teacher with the right message at the right time; and just as human and divine as the rest of us.
- Someone invented the idea that Jesus be literally "resurrected" because it fit into their agenda. (This is Paul's doctrine of atonement.) The real message should have been that Jesus' preaching and teachings were so powerful that, even though he was crucified "dead and buried," people felt he was still there with them.
- We have been led to believe that Jesus was born of a virgin (Mary had not had sex with Joseph), but we should have been taught that this story is a myth emphasizing the importance of his birth. These myths (Matthew tells one story and Luke a quite different one) are not historical facts.
- The church has taught us to believe that if one dares to think outside the box, then that person is not a Christian. The church should have been telling us that Jesus ended up on a cross because he thought outside the box about his religion, Judaism.
- The institution has told followers for centuries that such stories as the Immaculate Conception, walking on water, raising people from the dead and the many miracles are true. They should have told us the truth: These are simply myths used by the early church to emphasize the power of Jesus' message.
- Since the fourth century we have been led to believe that God wrote the Bible. We should have been told that the Bible was written by humans who felt they had a special relationship with God and wanted to tell the story from their bias.

- The doctrine of the Trinity has been taught for centuries. The church now needs to admit it is inadequate and get rid of it.

Because so many of these ideas have been promulgated by the church for so many centuries, perhaps some of you are wondering if you take away all these ancient ideas from the Christian faith will you have anything left? Good question and my feelings are "Yes, you definitely will. You will be able to find the heart of Jesus' message" and still be a Christian."

I realize I have been critical of the Roman Catholic Church, my own Episcopal Church, the fundamental/evangelical movement, organized Christianity in general and the institutional church. I am sorry if I have offended. That has not been my objective. My intention has been to share what I see happening in the church and to call attention to the fact that I see so much of the thinking of the institutional church as diametrically opposed to the teachings of Jesus. I see myself in an interesting place. Although I have been heavily involved in the church my whole life (except for a few years in college) my real commitment started when I went to seminary in 1957. I then worked inside the church for 15 years. The church was my life. In 1975 I was obliged to leave full time work in the church and become a part-time priest. I visited many churches. I saw how other clergy functioned. I stayed out of the politics of the church. Now my livelihood was not dependent on the church. I was able to think outside the box without having to worry about financial consequences. I could speak my true feelings without having to be silenced. Above all, for the first time I could see what was happening in and to the Episcopal church. It wasn't good and still isn't. The church is dying a slow death.

In the 1990s I became interested in "The Jesus Seminar," an international, interdenominational group of some 200 Biblical scholars who have shared their out of the box observations about Jesus, Paul and the early church. I have read their books, listened to their tapes and devoured their articles. I have started a small discussion group of those who want to investigate the writings of the scholars who are involved with this movement. One of my favorite magazines is published by the Jesus Seminar. It is called *"The 4th R."* (Reading, wRiting, aRithmetic and the fourth "R", Religion.) They publish six copies a year and every time one comes to our home, I usually read it within a day. The September-October 2005 issue had an article entitled, "Postmodernism, the Historical Jesus, and the Church," by David Galston, a Canadian pastor, scholar and radio host. Admittedly, the title did not attract me. It sounded dull. But I read on and once I arrived at the second page, I could not put it down. I underlined many of David's major points, but was fascinated by his admission that "what I learned in seminary was mainly how to lie." That struck a bell. That's me. That is what I did for so many years in the church: I promulgated the lies I was taught in seminary. About twenty years ago I knew I needed to stop lying, and needed to start telling the truth about the real Jesus. It was very different from what I had learned in seminary.

By no means am I alone in this quest. There are bishops, priests, clergy and lay people who are also searching for the real Jesus. Another well-known scholar, author, and Anglican priest (in forced retirement), Don Cupitt, has this to say about the subject: "The Church has distorted the message of Jesus and made him someone he never claimed to be, the divine pre-existent Logos. It has emphasized another heavenly world and a life of discipline under authority instead of the Kingdom of love and justice to be established here and now on earth." (Cupitt, ***"Post-Christianity,"*** pages 29-30). Cupitt calls Jesus "an ethical teacher."

Nigel Leaves, in his book, ***Surfing on the Sea of Faith, The Ethics and Religion of Dan Cupitt*** (Polebridge Press, Santa Rosa, CA 2005) shares another Cupitt thought, "Christianity isn't about saving one's soul, but about losing oneself in the work of love...Love saves the world and justifies the poor, the wicked and the ungodly. We have to do the work of God" (Cupitt, ***"After God***," page 128).

So many of us who have spent our adult lives in the church want the institution to start changing its direction. This can only begin when we stop spreading the lies and start telling the truth. Let's stop telling people that Jesus is arisen from the dead and start telling folks that Jesus is a radical charismatic revolutionary who wants his followers to live by The Great Commandment.

I still see Jesus' message as revolutionary. He started revolutionizing my life in 1957 when I started seminary and still continues to do so. I have seen the error of my ways and the damage I have done by perpetuating the lies and myths of the church. I have stopped.

I appreciate the way Bishop John Spong stated his thoughts in his book, ***The Sins of Scripture*** (Harper San Francisco 2005) "We are not fallen sinners who need to be rescued; we are incomplete creatures who need to be empowered to step into the new possibilities of an expanding life. It is not appropriate to wallow in our inadequacy or to accept as our due being designated by religion or having our behavior controlled or our guilt expanded. We do not need to be punished either in this life or in the life to come, nor do we need to have some mythical god figure take our punishment for us. What we need is the power to take the next step into a new and more complete humanity, to transcend our limits, to step across the self-erected boundaries of our insecure humanity." (page 179)

Here are the revolutionary messages I hear from Jesus and his friends: "You shall love the Lord your God with all your heart, and with all your soul, and with all your mind, and with all your strength. The second is like this, 'You shall love your neighbor as yourself.' ***There is no other commandment greater than this."*** (Mark 12:30)

For me, this is about as simple and direct as an order could be. I call this "my marching orders." To reinforce this idea I like Paul's quote I used at the start of this chapter, ***"Faith, hope, love abide, these three; but the greatest of these is love"*** (I Corinthians 13:13).

Judgment: "Why do you see the speck that is in your brother's eye, but do not notice the log that is in your own eye...You hypocrite, ***first take the log out of your own eye, and then you will see clearly to take the speck out of your brother's eye."*** (Matthew 7:3-5) It couldn't be too much clearer than this. But how come I never seem to be able to get the log out of my eye? I also appreciate the message in John 8:1-11 where some religious leaders brought a woman caught in the act of adultery to Jesus. They wanted to stone her to death. Jesus responds, ***"Let him who is without sin among you be the first to throw a stone at her."*** They all "went away." As soon as I become perfect, then I can start throwing stones. But that is not going to happen. My humanity keeps getting in the way.

Forgiveness: Peter wants to know "how often shall my brother sin against me, and I forgive him? As many as seven times?" Jesus replies, "I do not say to you seven times, but ***seventy times seven"*** (Matthew 18-21-22). That's rather simple: I am to forgive everyone for anything an infinite number of times. Just in case that is not direct enough, Jesus reminds us, "So if you are offering your gift at the altar, and there remember that your brother has something against you, leave your gift before the altar and go; ***first be reconciled with your brother, and then come and offer your gift"*** (Matthew 5:23). It simply states: "We must forgive." In the May 1, 2006 issue of "Bottom Line," there was an article entitled "Did You Know That It Really Pays to Forgive?" It goes on to say, "Remember that forgiveness is something you do for you."

Agape: The following command is extremely powerful for me, "When the Son of man comes...he will separate them one from another as a shepherd separates his sheep from the goats, and he will place a sheep at his right hand, but the goats at his left. Then the King will say to those at his right hand, "Come, O blessed of my Father, inherit the kingdom prepared for you from the foundation of the world; for I was hungry and you gave me food, I was thirsty and you gave me drink, I was a stranger and you welcomed me, I was naked and you clothed me, I was sick and you visited me, I was in prison and you came to me.' Then the righteous will answer him, 'Lord, when did we see you hungry and feed you, or thirsty and give you a drink? And when did we see you as a stranger and welcome you, or naked and clothe you? And when did we see you sick and in prison and visit you?' And the King will answer them, 'Truly, I say to you, ***as you did it to one of the least of these my brethren, you did it to me'"*** (John 25:31-46). This is not speculation about what future judgment at the Pearly Gates is going to bring us; rather it's a command from Jesus about how we are to take *agape* into the hurting world to make it a better place in which to live.

How does one find life? "Whoever would save his life [*by not loving*] will lose it; and ***whoever loses his life for my sake [by loving]*** and the Gospel's will save it" (Mark 12:35).

One of the most powerful Christmas cards we ever received was from a young woman who was volunteering in one of our ministries. She was going to school and didn't have much money so she made her own Christmas cards and wrote on them: ***"Christmas presence—give yourself away!"*** What a great summation about what we are to do with our lives!

How about this idea: ***"It is more blessed to give than to receive"*** (Acts 20:13).

Or this one: ***"Let all that you do be done in love***" (Romans 16:13). When I am tempted to blame others, I need to remember that, as I am pointing a finger at the other person, there are three pointing back at me. Ah yes, I need to get the log out of my eye before I try to get the speck out of yours.

I cannot forget ***"work out your own salvation with fear and trembling"*** (Philippians 2:12). I don't have to work out my wife's or our daughters' or anyone else's. I am responsible for me, just me. I do not need to tell others how to do it.

How about some constant reminders: I need to read, reread and reread again the parables about "The Good

Samaritan (Luke 10:29-37) or "The Prodigal Son" (Luke 15:11-32). These stories never get old. They are roadmaps about how we are to do life.

Again: "But the greatest of these is ***love.***" (I Corinthians 13:13b). In his great letter to the church in Rome Paul shares this idea; "Owe no one anything, except to love one another. For he who loves his neighbor has fulfilled the law. The commandments, "You shall not commit adultery; You shall not murder; You shall no steal; You shall not covet"; and any other commandments are summed up in these words: "Love your neighbor as yourself. Love does no wrong to a neighbor; therefore love is the fulfilling of the law" (Romans 13: 8-10). Could it be any clearer?

One of my favorite axioms forces me to move quickly to resolve issues: "Be angry but do not sin; ***do not let the sun go down on your anger"*** (Ephesians 4:26). Conflict must be resolved quickly or it grows worse by the moment.

The above sayings and parables give me so much more hope and power than does a physically resurrected Jesus who died because all of us are "miserable" and "wretched" human beings.

There was a Dilbert comic strip that spoke very loudly to me. It showed the little animal character sitting on Dilbert's bed and saying, "I decided to start a discount religion." Next strip: "The tithing would only be 5% and I'd let people sin as much as they wanted." The last one: "The only problem is that I don't want to spend any time with anyone who would join that sort of religion." That is how I feel. I don't want to spend any more time playing the game, retelling the lies and myths or trying to pretend that the church is relevant in our world. I want to be an agent of change.

One of my mantras in life is, I don't mind listening to a problem but please also present a solution. I have shared with you the problems I am seeing, and now would like to share with you what I see as the solution. It has to start with finding "again" the historical Jesus. Marcus Borg, in a title of one of his books, puts it very succinctly, ***Finding Jesus Again for the First Time.*** Jesus has already been found, thanks to the work that has been done by The Jesus Seminar. Their years of research have been culminated in a book called, ***The Acts of Jesus: What Did Jesus Really Do?"*** (Robert Funk and Jesus Seminar Scholars Polebridge Press, 1998). This book takes us to the beginning of our journey. It shows us who Jesus really was without all the added biases of time and those who wrote the Gospels. Now we meet a charismatic teacher with a very appealing message about love. This was his central theme. He was not about the next life in a fictitious heaven or hell. Jesus wanted to give his followers the key to doing life here. I believe that Jesus had no idea that the intense anger of the religious leaders was going to result in his being crucified. He knew he frustrated them, but I do not think for a moment Jesus thought they would put him on a cross because he opposed them. Maybe they might try to banish him or whip him, but not murder him. He had no concept of a physical resurrection. Most Jewish people were not into resurrection theology. Even Paul in his early writing did not foster such an idea. So let us put aside a physical resurrection and now look at Jesus, the man.

He was not a complex person but rather a man with a powerful, eternal message about love. His miracles taken in a literal sense make him look more like a first century Houdini than a great teacher. We need to look at the miracles with more of a figurative interpretation, asking, "What is the real meaning behind such stories?"

For example, let us look at the story of Jesus making water into wine as found in the early part of the Gospel of John (2:1-11). This is not a story about how great an enologist/wine maker Jesus was, but rather a reminder that Jesus' message is about taking the ordinary (the water) and making the extraordinary (good wine) out of it. This miracle story message for me is that the ethics of Jesus will make our ordinary lives into extraordinary lives. How does this happen?

At a certain stage in writing a book, some authors will send manuscripts to people who will read them and react. I did just that, and one of my readers returned the manuscript with the thought that the book challenged him but when he came to the end his question was, "Okay, I've read the book. What does Bil want me to do now?" I liked that feedback so let me share some ideas.

What you as an individual might do:

1. Make certain that you understand the concept of "*agape*" love. It demands a great deal but the rewards can change lives.
2. Ask yourself the hard question: "Do I love myself?" We are not talking about loving yourself in an egotistical way such as, "Mirror, mirror on the wall, who is fairest of them all?" And the answer is "Me!" Rather, do you love who you are (warts and all) because you are a Creature of Creation and have gifts? Again, we are not talking about "liking" yourself all the time. That is not going to happen. Everyone has moments when they are not pleased with themselves for some of the things they have done or not done. We all know that at times we could do a better job with life. Our job as followers is to love and accept who we are and go from there.

Suppose your answer is, I cannot love myself! I shall not allow me to love me. I am a "wretch!" The next step is to then figure out where and when you received that message. Was it a parental or family message that keeps replaying? Maybe someone was continually reminding you, "You'll never amount to anything!" "You're useless!" "You're a failure!" And you bought into it. In order to move ahead you need to erase that message, and if you cannot do it by yourself, seek the help of a professional.

Or perhaps your negative image is about an event in your life? I was a fat boy growing up and had such nicknames as "Fat-in-the-can," "Crisco Kid," "Jelly Belly," "Lard Butt" just to mention a few. Even though I am now slim and have been since 1956, at times I still feel fat. I know I am not, but the message is still there. Do you have a recurring message that prevents you from loving yourself?

Maybe you did a "not nice" in your past and you will not totally forgive yourself? My line of thinking goes like this: What I did in the past is done. I cannot undo it, but I can make amends, and move forward with my life in a positive and creative way. My life is about the future.

Is there some physical trait that prevents you from loving who you are? Because we have a daughter who was born deaf and legally blind, we have been involved in that community. Some people use their handicap as a crutch and play "poor me." Others move beyond that. We have met deaf/blind people who are extremely successful. One man who is deaf/blind not only owns his own restaurant, but is also the chef. Then there is Helen Keller who is a legend because she refused to believe that her "challenges" should hold her back. Other deaf/blind people are directors of statewide rehabilitation services. Some are principals of schools for the deaf and deaf/blind. They have staff with dual sensory impairments. So one needs to ask oneself: What physical or mental limitation could prevent a person from achieving his or her dreams? There are people such as Ray Charles (blind musician), Franklin D. Roosevelt (President of the United States who had polio), Christopher Reeve (actor who became a paraplegic after an accident), Stevie Wonder (blind musician) and many others who refused to allow a handicap to stop them from being who they wanted to be.

I have discovered that if people cannot love themselves fully and completely, they cannot fully or completely love their neighbor or their Creator.

3. If we are to love ourselves and our neighbor we need to come to grips with our prejudices, biases or even hatreds. There is no human being who is free from prejudices. Granted, there are some people who handle their biases better than others, but we all have them. Therefore one needs to make a list of those prejudices. Perhaps it is people from another race, culture or social class? I was surprised when we came to California in 1975, how many Californians had strong feelings about or against

Hispanics. On the other hand, these same people would allow them to clean their houses, take care of their yards, clean their pools and babysit their children. I thought this rather strange.

Politically, I also think outside the box. Many folks think I am a Democrat because I do believe in social justice. But some Republicans believe I am one of them because I am for less government and fewer taxes. (I worked for government for 15 years and saw first-hand our tax money being wasted.) To be honest, I do not think I am for either party. But what fascinates me is how many people refuse to talk about religion, politics or sex. The only reason I can garner is that people become so polarized (perhaps a nicer word for prejudiced) and passionate, that they are not able to even have a discussion about other points of view. I love to discuss. How else can I hear new ideas? Are your biases so strong about politics, religion and sex that you cannot talk about them, especially with someone with whom you might not agree? That is a prejudice.

Go over your list of those for whom you might have a prejudice. Have you considered an ex-spouse, former friend, the police or those in authority? Gays? Lesbians? Transvestites? Obese people? Street people? Drug addicts? The rich? The poor? Academicians? The illiterate? Immigrants, especially illegal ones?

Whatever the issues are, we need to come to identify, understand and be continually aware of them. If we don't, we find ourselves being rather selective as to whom our neighbor is and we are not free to love, accept and forgive them. Does this mean that I cannot live *agape* love until I am totally free of all prejudices? No, because that is humanly impossible. This simply means that I need to know that I have preconceived notions about people that could get in the way of my loving that person. For example, if one feels uncomfortable (another word for prejudice) about street people, then perhaps one should volunteer in a homeless shelter and meet some of the clients. Granted, some are scary, but so many who use this service are good people, just down on their luck. Sometimes simply showing our love and concern for these folks could be the deciding factor that gets them off the street. Remember the Good Samaritan?

4. Let us address the issue of challenging intolerance. Some see this as being diametrically opposed to the ethics of Jesus. We must be tolerant, even of people's intolerance. However I have found that when I am tolerant of other people's prejudices, it is sort of like giving them permission to be intolerant. If I let them know directly that their prejudice(s) makes me uncomfortable, then they understand my stance. If they decide to write me off as a friend/acquaintance, then I have to make that their problem. This does not mean that I do not love that person or that I need to make him/her an enemy. As a follower, we have to love, accept, forgive everyone, but we cannot ignore intolerance.

I have a cousin who has a son who is gay. This son is a very successful businessman, a great uncle to his nephews and nieces, a caring loving son/brother and a wonderful human being. My cousin worked in an office where another man, having no idea that my cousin had a son who was gay, would constantly make disparaging remarks about gays. My cousin and I talked about the situation and I suggested that every time the man made a negative remark, my cousin would openly express his discomfort. Very quickly, the man received the message and was most apologetic. Never again was a disparaging remark made about gays. Challenging intolerance works. It allows one to confront prejudices in a loving but no-nonsense way.

5. Another question people have asked me is: Can one be a non-Christian and still subscribe to the ethics of Jesus? The simple answer is, of course one can. After all, Jesus was not a Christian. He was Jewish from birth to death and he certainly practiced what he preached. When I was doing inter-faith work in the 1990s, I would often sit on inter-faith panels where we would discuss our different beliefs. The most interesting thing was as each panel member would give a brief summary of his or her belief

system, love was always at the center. However, I have never spoken with an atheist or agnostic about their ethical system so I really don't know if they would feel comfortable using the ethics of Jesus, but they certainly could if they so desired.

Whatever one's belief system, I do know that the ethics of Jesus are not as easy to put into practice as they might sound. Because there are only limited guidelines, one must be willing to make decisions and live with the consequences. For me, the ethics of Jesus is a way of life that requires study (the Bible, books and articles about ethics), evaluation and making constant corrections. I find in my own life that I am continually falling back into my old ways of doing life with its prejudices, negative judgments, intolerances and unloving actions. I know that I shall never totally master the ethics of Jesus. I must make adjustments. So whether one is a Christian, or of another faith or of no specific faith system, one needs to realize that adhering to this ethical system is not necessarily easy.

The ethics of Jesus and the family

If one wants to include the ethics of Jesus in their family life, there need to be two adults committed to the process. It can work in a home where there is only one adult present, but that adult must be willing to work extra hard at the process. The two adult family helps to keep both parents on target. Adults need to model the process, which means that both people have come to terms with their own prejudices and biases. Their relationship has to be such that the adults are able to keep each other honest. If mistakes are made, then they must be discussed and corrected. This is not always an easy thing to do. Sometimes when my wife points out my inconsistencies underneath I resent it, but she is inevitably right and I need to make the necessary adjustments.

I think it is important for children to see their parents have an argument. How else can children learn that not only is it acceptable for people to disagree, but also how they resolve those disagreements and still continue to love one another? Parents who always take their arguments into a private place are not helping children to learn resolution skills. For children to see their parents in conflict and then witness forgiveness, acceptance and love is a great lesson learned.

Suppose the adults are not able to resolve a conflict, what should they do? My solution would be to seek help from a third unbiased party. As I have told you, we are the parents of a child with multiple challenges. Children without such challenges are difficult enough to raise, but a child with handicaps is quite a challenge to a marriage. In our daughter's early years, my wife and I had a constant struggle going. She was willing to excuse some of our daughter's weaknesses because of her handicaps. My theory was that in the real world most people are not very tolerant of weaknesses and that our daughter had to face up to them. It was a struggle between her being too soft versus my hardnosed Marine tactics. Occasionally, we needed a third party to help us move through this struggle. But it worked and our daughters were able to see two people struggle with conflict, but end up being happily married and in love.

How do the ethics of Jesus work with two adults going through a divorce? As I have suggested before, I believe divorce is a necessary option for people who have fallen out of love and do not want to spend the rest of their lives living in a negative situation. I do not think it is healthy for the adults and it can be very damaging for children to live in an atmosphere with two people who are not able to model love. As a therapist, when I saw two people who were at odds with each other and they could not or would not make the necessary changes to make the relationship work, I would recommend a separation period, individual counseling and perhaps later, couples counseling. It is not easy to repair problems in a marriage, especially if these difficulties have gone on for any length of time. If I could see that a separation and counseling were not working, then we would talk about divorce. At that stage, I would then strongly recommend a divorce mediator rather than an attorney. Too often I have seen attorneys who keep the conflict constantly stirred up with their arbitrary ways. Divorce mediators, often therapists, manage to find areas of common agreement and then simply mediate the relatively few areas of disagreement. I find this approach much less hostile so each of the divorced parties ends up with some dignity…and money.

As parents and followers of the ethics of Jesus, I think it is important to instill the basic concept of the ethics of Jesus into our children. This starts with modeling acceptance of all and instant forgiveness as the children run into conflicts with schoolmates, siblings, neighborhood children and relatives. The "hate" word needs to be just as forbidden as foul language. Children must not be allowed to use pejorative or negative expressions about another race, culture or religion. Nor can their friends be allowed to display such negative behavior. Again, this is not easy, especially as our children grow into their teenage years and are influenced by the prejudices of their friends.

Sometimes parents "protect" their children from those who are different from us so the children never have an opportunity to deal with street people, those from other cultures, religions or someone with an alternative lifestyle. It was interesting to watch other children deal with our daughter who was challenged. Some were terrified of her because she walked differently (she has mild cerebral palsy) or her deaf speech or eyes that did not track correctly. She would stare at people trying to figure out who they were. Many ignored her because they did not know how to deal with her. When I was the director of the church camp, our family would stay at the camp all summer. We would put this daughter into a cabin group for a week with other campers who were not challenged. Her counselor and cabin group worked very hard at communicating with her and making her a part of the group. There was a tremendous learning curve for the staff, her fellow campers and others at camp. The "fear" of dealing with a person who was different went to almost zero. There were even a few who met our daughter at camp, became fascinated with sign language, and went on to become teachers for the hearing impaired.

The real world is vastly different from our little niche of family and friends, so to expose our children to the other different world is doing them a great service. The end result will be an understanding of people who are not just like us and eliminate prejudices based on ignorance and a lack of understanding.

As grandparents, we have an even better opportunity to help our grandchildren appreciate the world in which they live. For my wife and me, one of the better inheritances we can give and show our children and grandchildren is the gift of understanding how one could live their life being a follower of the ethics of Jesus. We need to challenge their prejudices, to give them an opportunity to, and if possible, live with people who are different from us or have alternative life styles. Perhaps we can be more accepting and not so critical/judgmental of our grandchildren. We need to show them the way and let our actions of *agape* tell the story.

The Great Commandment states that we are to love our self, our neighbor and Creator/Creation. In my estimation, one of the better ways one can show love to God or Creation/Creator is by appreciating and respecting the environment in which we live. The Industrial Age has not been very friendly to Creation on this planet. We are finding that our disrespect for the Creation and the resulting pollution has done irreparable damage to this earth and perhaps the universe. Adherents to the ethics of Jesus can help reverse this trend, even if only in small ways by doing such things as turning off water faucets rather than allowing them to continually run as we brush our teeth or shave. The same is true when we conserve electricity by turning off our switches. The recycling of our trash is extremely important. I am always amazed on "trash day" how many people do not recycle, especially now that our cities have made it so simple. We can ride our bikes or walk instead of always hopping in the car. Or we can purchase automobiles that are environmentally friendly. These are just a few of the small things one can do to show our respect for Creation.

We live in a beach community that has one of the more polluted ocean waters in all of California. Our city is working diligently to correct this problem and has made great strides in keeping runoff water from entering the ocean. They are also requesting residents to join in this battle and are asking us not to over-water our lawns, not to wash cars in the streets, to keep polluting chemicals off our lawns and out of our sewage, and to clean up dog feces. This endeavor to save our ocean has cost the residents big tax dollars, but the end results have been worth it. The rating for our ocean pollution has gone from an "F" to an "A," the marine life is flourishing and swimmers/surfers are not being infected with strange bacteria. This has happened primarily because the people of our community are dedicated to respecting the environment and, from my perspective, showing their love of Creation. The ethics of Jesus demand that we be good stewards of our environment in our homes, our communities, our countries and the universe.

The ethics of Jesus and the work world

When we first moved to California in 1975 and I was not able to be a full time clergyman, I went to work for a small city as the Director of Human Services. It was my job to design and implement a human services delivery system. This took about three years and after that time I found I was bored. My creative juices were not challenged. After many months with a professional guidance counseling service, I was told that I should go into business for myself. This was a scary idea (I was trained to be a pastor, not a businessman), but after my wife and I wrestled with the idea I/we decided I should give it a try. Thus, the birth of our new company, "People Helpers, Inc." whose mission was to contract with public and private agencies to provide human services, recreation services and childcare. Within a few years we had a million dollar a year business with 125 employees. I honestly tried to incorporate the ethics of Jesus into my business, but I can assure you that it was not always easy, especially since I was contracting with agencies that were not at all interested in operating that way. (It was my conclusion then, and still is, that one can ***not*** be in politics and be an adherent to the ethics of Jesus. This is a sad commentary on our political system.)

But we gave it our best shot. There was profit sharing. Staff meetings were meant to keep the air clear of biases and prejudices. We had a multi-cultural staff. Our benefits package was like a buffet. Staff could pick and choose the benefits they needed, not simply ones the company thought they needed. We tried not to fire people, but rather to work with them so that they could do a better job at their task. Being a businessman trying to practice the ethics of Jesus was a challenge. I seemed to be constantly putting out fires so that they would not get out of control. The bottom line is that I think the work-a-day world and the ethics of Jesus are compatible.

At times when one reads the newspaper, one wonders if the business world has any ethics at all. Greed seems to be kingpin. But I am also noticing how some companies are now giving a course in ethics to new hires. Recently, in the business section of our local paper there was a feature section on all the local resources for business people such as "The Center for Faith and Business," "Connecting Business Men to Christ," the "Christian Management Association" to mention just a few of the ten agencies listed. I think there is now a renewed awareness of the importance of businesses having and adhering to a faith based ethical system.

The ethics of Jesus and our houses of worship

Let us now look at what we might do in our churches, temples, mosques or any house of worship.

- Most religious institutions have a mission statement reminding their members why they are there and what they are to do. The first question is: have you ever seen such a statement? If so, is it inclusive of everyone? Does it talk about love, acceptance and forgiveness? Could it ever be construed as being exclusive? Does it refer to The Great Commandment? I believe that a church without a clear-cut mission statement could easily be steered off course from what it is that Jesus wants us to do.

- Every church has a group of either chosen or elected members who are responsible for overseeing their church. Do you know who these people are? Would you be willing to ask them if, when they make decisions, are their decisions based on the ethics of Jesus? If not, what ethical system do they use? It has been my experience that often people who are in charge of running churches make their decisions based more on how a business would be run, rather than an ethical standard based on the ethics of Jesus. There is a huge difference between these two systems. One is based on the "bottom line" while the other is based on love.
- Have you ever examined the annual budget of your house of worship? This is where one can tell what a church actually believes. How much of their annual budget is spent on keeping their church going versus what is being spent on reaching out to the hurting world? My findings over the years are that most Episcopal churches spend about 5 to 20% of their budget on outreach. The rest is spent on themselves, paying salaries and mortgages on buildings. In the New Testament I have never read about Jesus suggesting that His Kingdom is built around buildings, paid staff, fancy organs or expensive appointments. But over and over I hear his message about loving people.
- In one of the parishes in which I was involved, the governing body worked diligently at attaining the goal that 50% of their money would be spent on

keeping the church building and staff going, but the other 50% would be spent on ministry to the hurting world. The most interesting thing about this approach was the more outreach was stressed and made top priority, the more people pledged and new members joined. Americans are generous givers, especially if they feel that what they give is going to causes that help to make this a better world in which to live.

- How often, if ever, have you heard your spiritual leader preach and/or teach about the ethics of Jesus or The Great Commandment? I suspect the answer might be, "Not often" or "Never." Perhaps you could ask your leader to preach about The Great Commandment or to teach a class about the ethics of Jesus. This should not be too difficult to do. The New Testament is full of resource material.
- Does your religious institution ever discuss the concept of being stewards of Creation? This is a sermon I have never heard preached: How each of us has a responsibility to take excellent care of our universe- if we truly love God or Creation/Creator. The institutional church needs to be the leader in preserving our environment.

My belief is that once the mainstream churches start to understand and put into practice the ethics of Jesus, that will be the time when they will start to become alive and relevant again. Doctrine, liturgy, building buildings and maintaining the institution will start to take a back seat to our going into the real world to tackle such issues as poverty, racism, sexism, and all the other "-isms." People once again will be attracted to churches because they are relevant and leading the charge for social justices.

When people see the church living "The Great Commandment," they will also want to start doing the same in their own lives. One of the more Jesus-centered churches I ever attended was in southern California. It was not a huge church and had maybe 250 active members. This little parish had over 40 ministries both within and outside the church. The ministries were in the local community, the county, other states in the USA and around the world. New ministries were constantly being developed while old ones were being evaluated as to their effectiveness. It was fascinating watching new people come into the church and being attracted to the ministries. Their lives were transformed. The spirit of loving becomes contagious. Occasionally, I would stand in front of the congregation and talk about a cause that needed money, or we needed diapers for a single mom, furniture for a family moving to bigger quarters or some expertise had by some of the members. Inevitably, what I was asking for came forth. It was a parish in which people were constantly challenged to share their time, talent and treasure, and they did.

My dream is that this little book will start you thinking about the powerful impact that the ethics of Jesus can make on our individual lives as well as that of the institutional church. I have seen what his ethics have done to my life. It has been transformed. I have seen churches that have heard the message and I have seen their great transformation. To me, the ethics of Jesus are much more powerful than a resurrection theology. A man arising from the dead does little for me. A gospel of love, which has figurative "resurrection" qualities, makes my life exhilarating and exciting. Try it. You'll love it.

APPENDIX

Chapter 2, ***THEOLOGICALLY SPEAKING...***

1. Matthew 13:55 and 56

   "Is not this the carpenter's son? Is not his mother called Mary? And are not his brothers James and Joseph and Simon and Judas? And are not all his sisters with us? Where then did this man get all this?"

   Mark 6:3

   "Is not this the carpenter, the son of Mary and brother of James and Joses and Judas and Simon, and are not his sisters here with us? And they took offense at him."

2. Mark 16:1-8

   When the Sabbath was over, Mary Magdalene, and Mary the mother of James, and Salome brought spices, so that they might go and anoint him. And very early on the first day of the week, when the sun had risen, they went to the tomb. They had been saying to one another, "Who will roll away the stone for us from the entrance to the tomb?" When the looked up, they saw that the stone, which was very large, had already been rolled back. As they entered the tomb, they saw a young man, dressed in a white robe, sitting on the right side; and they were alarmed. But he said to them, "Do not be alarmed; you are looking for Jesus of Nazareth, who was crucified. He has been raised; he is not here. Look, there is the place they laid him. But go, tell his disciples and Peter that he is going ahead of you to Galilee; there you will see him, just as he told you." So they went out and fled froM the tomb, for terror and amazement had seized them; and they said nothing to anyone, for they were afraid.

Chapter 3, ***WHAT JESUS' ETHICS AREN'T!***

1. Exodus 20:1-17

Then God spoke all these words: I am the Lord your God, who brought you out of the land of Egypt, out of the house of slavery; you shall have no other gods before me.

You shall not make for yourself an idol, whether in the form of anything that is in heaven above, or that is on the earth beneath, or that is in the water under the earth. You shall not bow down to them or worship them; for I the Lord your God am a jealous God, punishing children for the iniquity of parents, to the third and the fourth generation of those who reject me, but showing steadfast love to the thousandth generation of those who love me and keep my commandments.

You shall not make wrongful use of the name of the Lord your God, for the Lord will not acquit anyone who misuses his name.

Remember the Sabbath day, and keep it holy. Six days you shall labor and do all your work. But the seventh day is a Sabbath to the Lord your God; you shall not do any work—you, your son or your daughter, your male or female slave, your livestock, or the alien resident in your towns. For in six days the Lord made heaven and earth, the sea, and all that is in them, but rested the seventh day; therefore the Lord blessed the Sabbath day and consecrated it.

Honor your father and your mother, so that your days may be long in the land that the Lord your God is giving you.

You shall not murder.

You shall not commit adultery.

You shall not steal.

You shall not bear false witness against your neighbor.

You shall not covet your neighbor's house; you shall not covet your neighbor's wife, or male or female slave, or ox, or donkey, or anything that belongs to your neighbor.

Deuteronomy 5:1-21

Moses convened all Israel, and said to them:

Hear, O Israel, the statutes and ordinances that I am addressing to you today; you shall learn them and observe them diligently. The Lord our God made a covenant with us at Horeb. Not with our ancestors did the Lord make this covenant, but with us, who are all of us here alive today. The Lord spoke with you face to face at the mountain, out of the fire. (At that time I was standing between the Lord and you to declare to you the words of the Lord; for you were afraid because of the fire and did not go up the mountain). And he said:

I am the Lord your God, who brought you out of the land of Egypt, out of the house of slavery; you shall have no other gods before me.

You shall not make for yourself an idol, whether in the form of anything that is in the heaven above, or that is on the earth beneath, or that is in the water under the earth. You shall not bow down to them or worship them; for I the Lord your God am a jealous God, punishing children for the iniquity of parents, to the third and fourth generation of those who reject me, but showing steadfast love to the thousandth generation of those who love me and keep my commandments.

You shall not make wrongful use of the name of the Lord your God, for the Lord will not acquit anyone who misuses his name.

Observe the Sabbath day and keep it holy, as the Lord your God commanded you. Six days you shall labor and do all your work. But the seventh day is a Sabbath to the Lord your God; you shall not do any work—you, or your son or your daughter, or your male or female slave, or your ox or your donkey, or any of your livestock, or the resident alien in your towns, so that your male and female slave may rest as well as you. Remember that you were a slave in the land of Egypt, and the Lord your God brought you out from there with a mighty hand and an outstretched arm; therefore the Lord your God commanded you to keep the Sabbath day.

Honor your father and your mother, as the Lord your God commanded you, so that your days may be long and that it may go well with you in the land that the Lord your God is giving you.

You shall not murder.

Neither shall you commit adultery.

Neither shall you steal.

Neither shall you bear false witness against your neighbor.

Neither shall you covet your neighbor's wife.

Neither shall you desire your neighbor's house, or field, or male or female slave, or ox, or donkey, or anything that belongs to your neighbor.

2. Matthew 19:18

He said to him, "Which ones?" And Jesus said, "You shall not murder; You shall not commit adultery; You shall not steal; You shall not bear false witness."

Mark 10:19

"You know the commandments: 'You shall not murder; You shall not commit adultery; You shall not steal; You shall not bear false witness; You shall not defraud; Honor your father and mother.'"

Luke 18:20

"You know the commandments: "'You shall not commit adultery; You shall not murder; You shall not steal; You shall not bear false witness; Honor your father and mother.'"

3. Matthew 5:3-12

"Blessed are the poor in spirit, for theirs is the kingdom of heaven.

"Blessed are those who mourn, for they will be comforted.

"Blessed are the meek, for they will inherit the earth.

"Blessed are those who hunger and thirst for righteousness, for they will be filled.

"Blessed are the merciful, for they will receive mercy.

"Blessed are the pure in heart, for they will see God.

"Blessed are the peacemakers, for they will be called children of God.

"Blessed are those who are persecuted for righteousness' cake, for theirs is the kingdom of heaven.

"Blessed are you when people revile you and persecute you and utter all kinds of evil against you falsely on my account. Rejoice and be glad, for your reward is great in heaven, for in the same way they persecuted the prophets who were before you."

Luke 6:20-23

Then he looked up at his disciples and said:

"Blessed are you who are poor, for yours is the kingdom of God.

"Blessed are you who are hungry now, for you will be filled.

"Blessed are you who weep now, for you will laugh.

"Blessed are you when people hate you, and when they exclude you, revile you, and defame you on account of the Son of Man. Rejoice in that day and leap for joy, for surely your reward is great in heaven; for that is what their ancestors did to the prophets.

4. Matthew 5:31-32

"It was also said, 'Whoever divorces his wife, let him give her a certificate of divorce.' But I say to you that anyone who divorces his wife, except on the ground of unchastity, causes her to commit adultery; and whoever marries a divorced woman commits adultery."

Matthew 19:9

"And I say to you, whoever divorces his wife, except for unchastity, and marries another commits adultery."

5. Mark 10:11-12

He said to them, "Whoever divorces his wife and marries another commits adultery against her; and if she divorces her husband and marries another, she commits adultery."

6. Luke 16:18

"Anyone who divorces his wife and marries another commits adultery, and whoever marries a woman divorced from her husband commits adultery."

7. Matthew 5:38-42

"You have heard that it was said, 'An eye for an eye and a tooth for a tooth." But I say to you, Do not resist an evildoer. But if anyone strikes you on the right cheek, turn the other also; and if anyone wants to sue you and take your coat, give your cloak as well; and if anyone forces you to go one mile, go also the second mile. Give to everyone who begs from you, and do not refuse anyone who wants to borrow from you.

Luke 6:29-30

If anyone strikes you on the cheek, offer the other also; and for anyone who takes away your coat do not withhold even your shirt. Give to everyone who begs from you; and if anyone takes away your goods, do not ask for them again."

8. Ephesians 5:24

Just as the church is subject to Christ, so also wives ought to be, in everything, to their husbands.

9. I Corinthians 11:6

For if a woman will not veil herself, then she should cut off her hair; but if it is disgraceful for a woman to have her hair cut off or to be shaved, she should wear a veil.

10. I Corinthians 14:34

.... women should be silent in the churches. But they are not permitted to speak, but should be subordinate, as the law also says.

11. Ephesians 6:1

Children, obey your parents in the Lord, for this is right.

12. Ephesians 6:5

Slaves, obey your earthly masters with fear and trembling, in singleness of heart, as you obey Christ;

13. Romans 1:26

For this reason, God gave them up to degrading passions. Their women exchanged natural intercourse for unnatural,...

14. I Corinthians 6:9-10

Do you not know that wrongdoers will not inherit the kingdom of God? Do not be deceived! Fornicators, idolaters, adulterers, male prostitutes, sodomites, thieves, the greedy, drunkards, revilers, robbers—none of these will inherit the kingdom of God.

15. I Corinthians 13:1-13

If I speak in the tongues of mortals and of angels, but do not have love, I am a noisy gong or a clanging cymbal. And if I have prophetic powers, and understand all mysteries and all knowledge, and if I have all faith, so as to remove mountains, but do not have love, I am nothing. If I give away all my possessions, and if I hand over my body so that I may boast, but do not have love, I gain nothing.

Love is patient; love is kind; love is not envious or boastful or arrogant or rude. It does not insist on its own way; it is not irritable or resentful; it does not rejoice in wrong doing, but rejoices in the truth. It bears all things, believes all things, hopes all things, endures all things.

Love never ends. But as for prophecies, they will come to an end; as for tongues, they will cease; as for knowledge, it will come to an end. For we know only in part, and we prophesy only in part; but when the complete comes, the partial will come to an end.

When I was a child, I spoke like a child; when I became an adult, I put an end to childish ways. For now we see in a mirror, dimly, but then we will see face to face. Now I know only in part; then I will know fully, even as I have been fully known. And now faith, hope, and love abide, these three; and the greatest of these is love.

16. Matthew 23:1-39

Then Jesus said to the crowds and to his disciples, "The scribes and the Pharisees sit on Moses' seat; therefore, do whatever they teach you and follow it; but do not do as they do, for they do not practice what they teach. They tie up heavy burdens, hard to bear, and lay them on the shoulders of others; but they themselves are unwilling to lift a finger to move them. They do all their deeds to be seen by others; for they make their phylacteries broad and their fringes long. They love to have the place of honor at banquets and the best seats in the synagogues, and to be greeted with respect in the marketplaces, and to have people call them rabbi. But you are not to be called rabbi, for you have one teacher, and you are all students and call no one your father on earth, for you have one Father—the one in heaven. Nor are you to be called instructors, for you have one instructor, the Messiah.

The greatest among you will be your servant. All who exalt themselves will be humbled, and all who humble themselves will be exalted.

"But woe to you, scribes and Pharisees, hypocrites! For you lock people out of the kingdom of heaven. For you do not go in yourselves, and when others are going in, you stop them. Woe to you, scribes and Pharisees, hypocrites! For you cross sea and land to make a single convert, and you make the new convert twice as much a child of hell as yourselves.

"Woe to you, blind guides, who say, 'Whoever swears by the sanctuary is bound by nothing, but whoever swears by the gold of the sanctuary is bound by the oath.' You blind fools! For which is greater, the gold or the sanctuary that has made the gold sacred?

"And you say, 'Whoever swears by the altar is bound by nothing, but whoever swears by the gift that is on the altar is bound by the oath.' How blind you are! For which is greater, the gift or the altar that makes the gift sacred? So whoever swears by the altar, swears by it and by everything on it; and whoever swears by the sanctuary, swears by it and by the one who dwells in it; and whoever swears by heaven, swears by the throne of God and by the one who is seated upon it.

"Woe to you, scribes and Pharisees, hypocrites! For you tithe mint, dill, and cumin, and have neglected the weightier matters of the law: justice and mercy and faith. It is these you ought to have practiced without neglecting the others. You blind guides! You strain out a gnat but swallow a camel!

"Woe to you, scribes and Pharisees, hypocrites! For you clean the outside of the cup and of the plate, but inside they are full of greed and self-indulgence. You blind Pharisees! First clean the inside of the cup, so that the outside also may become clean.

"Woe to you, scribes and Pharisees, hypocrites! For you are like whitewashed tombs, which on the outside look beautiful, but inside they are full of the bones of the dead and of all kinds of filth. So you also on the outside look righteous to others, but inside you are full of hypocrisy and lawlessness.

"Woe to you, scribes and Pharisees, hypocrites! For you build the tombs of the prophets and decorate the graves of the righteous, and you say, 'If we had lived in the days of our ancestors, we would not have taken part with them in shedding the blood of the prophets.' Thus you testify against yourselves that you are descendants of those who murdered the prophets. Fill up, then, the measure of your ancestors. You snakes, you brood of vipers! How can you escape being sentenced to hell? Therefore I send you prophets, sages, and scribes, some of whom you will kill and crucify, and some you will flog in your synagogues and pursue from town to town, so that upon you may come all the righteous blood shed on earth, from the blood of righteous Abel to the blood of Zechariah son of Barachiah, whom you murdered between the sanctuary and the altar.

"Truly I tell you, all this will come upon this generation.

"Jerusalem, Jerusalem, the city that kills the prophets and stones those who are sent to it! How often have I desired to gather your children together as a hen gathers her brood under her wings, and you were not willing! See, your house is left to you, desolate. For I tell you, you will not see me again until you say, 'Blessed is the one who comes in the name of the Lord.'"

17. Luke 4:16-30

When he came to Nazareth, where he had been brought up, he went to the synagogue on the Sabbath day, as was his custom. He stood up and read, and the scroll of the prophet Isaiah was given to him. He unrolled the scroll and found the place where it was written:

"The Spirit of the Lord is upon me, because he has anointed me to bring good news to the poor.

He has sent me to proclaim release to the captives and recovery of sight to the blind, to let the oppressed go free, to proclaim the year of the Lord's favor."

And he rolled up the scroll, gave it back to the attendant, and sat down. The eyes of all in the synagogue were fixed on him. Then he began to say to them, "Today this scripture has been fulfilled in your hearing." All spoke well of him and were amazed at the gracious words that came from his mouth. They said, "Is not this Joseph's son?" He said to them, "Doubtless you will quote to me this proverb, 'Doctor, cure yourself.' And you will say, 'Do here also in your hometown the things that we have heard you did at Capernaum.' And he said, "Truly I tell you, no prophet is accepted in the prophet's hometown. But the truth is, there were many widows in Israel in the time of Elijah, when the heaven was shut up three years and six months, and there was a severe famine over all the land; yet Elijah was sent to none of them except to a widow at Zarephath in Sidon. There were also many lepers in Israel in the time of the prophet Elisha, and none of them was cleansed except Naaman the Syrian. When they heard this, all in the synagogue were filled with rage. They got up, drove him out of the town, and led him to the brow of the hill on which their town was built, so they might hurl him off the cliff. But he passed through the midst of them and went on his way.

Chapter 4. ***THE ETHICS OF JESUS***

1. Matthew 22:34-40

When the Pharisees heard that he had silenced the Sadducees, they gathered together, and one of them, a lawyer, asked him a question to test him. "Teacher, which commandment in the law is the greatest?" He said to him, "'You shall love the Lord your God with all your heart, and with all your soul, and with all your mind.' This is the greatest and first commandment. and a second is like it:

‘You shall love your neighbor as yourself.’ On these two commandments hang all the law and the prophets.”

Mark 12:28-31

One of the scribes came near and heard them disputing with one another, and seeing that he answered them well, he asked him, “Which commandment is the first of all?” Jesus answered, “The first is, ‘Hear, O Israel: the Lord our God, the Lord is one; you shall love the Lord your God with all your heart, and with all your soul, and with all your mind, and with all your strength.’ The second is this, ‘You shall love your neighbor as yourself.’ There is no other commandment greater than these.”

Luke 10:25-28

Just then a lawyer stood up to test Jesus. “Teacher,” he said, “what must I do to inherit eternal life?” He said to him, “What is written in the law? What do you read there?” He answered, ‘You shall love the Lord your God with all your heart, and with all your soul, and with all your strength, and with all your mind; and your neighbor as yourself.” And he said to him, “You have given the right answer; do this, and you will live.”

2. Matthew 5:43-48

“You have heard that it was said, ‘You shall love your neighbor and hate your enemy.’ But I say to you, Love your enemies and pray for those who persecute you, so that you may be children of your Father in heaven; for he makes his sun rise on the evil and on the good, and sends rain on the righteous and on the unrighteous. For if you love those who love you, what reward do you have? Do not even the tax collectors do the same? And if you greet only your brothers and sisters, what more are you doing than others? Do not even the Gentiles do the same? Be perfect, therefore, as your heavenly Father is perfect.”

Luke 6:27-28

"Woe to you when all speak well of you, for that is what their ancestors did to the false prophets.

"But I say to you that listen, Love your enemies, do good to those who hate you, bless those who curse you, pray for those who abuse you."

3. Mark 7:1-10

After Jesus had finished all his sayings in the hearing of the people, he entered Capernaum. A centurion there had a slave whom he valued highly; and who was ill and close to death. When he heard about Jesus, he sent some Jewish elders to him, asking him to come and heal his slave. When they came to Jesus, they appealed to him earnestly, saying, "He is worthy of having you do this for him, for he loves our people, and it is he who built our synagogue for us." And Jesus went with them, but when he was not far from the house, the centurion sent friends to say to him, "Lord, do not trouble yourself, for I am not worthy to have you come under my roof; therefore I did not presume to come to you. But only speak the word, and let my servant be healed. For I also am a man set under authority, with soldiers under me; and I say to one, 'Go,' and he goes, and to another, 'Come,' and he comes, and to my slave, 'Do this,' and the slave does it." When Jesus heard this he was amazed at him, and turning to the crowd that followed him, he said, "I tell you, not even in Israel have I found such faith." When those who had been sent returned to the house, they found the slave in good health.

Chapter 6, ***JESUS AND HIS FRIENDS TALK ABOUT LOVE***

1. Luke 15:11-32

Then Jesus said, "There was a man who had two sons. The younger of them said to his father, 'Father, give me the share of the property that will belong to me.'

So he divided his property between them. A few days later the younger son gathered all he had and traveled to a distant country, and there he squandered his property in dissolute living. When he had spent everything, a severe famine took place throughout the country, and he began to be in need. So he went and hired himself out to one of the citizens of that country, who sent him to his fields to feed the pigs. He would gladly have filled himself with the pods that the pigs were eating; and no one gave him anything. But when he came to himself he said, 'How many of my father's hired hands have bread enough and to spare, but here I am dying of hunger!

I will get up and go to my father, and I will say to him, "Father, I have sinned against heaven and before you; I am no longer worthy to be called your son; treat me like one of your hired hands."' So he set off and went to his father. But while he was still far off, his father saw him and was filled with compassion; he ran and put his arms around him and kissed him. Then the son said to him, 'Father, I have sinned against heaven and before you; I am no longer worthy to be called your son.' But the father said to his slaves, 'Quickly, bring out a robe—the best one—and put it on him; put a ring on his finger and sandals on his feet. And get the fatted calf and kill it, and let us eat and celebrate; for this son of mine was dead and is alive again; he was lost and is found!' And they began to celebrate."

2. Luke 10:29-37

But wanting to justify himself, he asked Jesus, "And who is my neighbor?" Jesus replied, "A man was going down from Jerusalem to Jericho, and fell into the hands of robbers, who stripped him, beat him, and went away, leaving him half dead. Now by chance a priest was going down that road and when he saw him, he passed by on the other side. So likewise a Levite, when he came to the place and saw him, passed by on the other side. But a Samaritan while traveling came near him; and when he saw him he was moved with pity. He went to him and bandaged his wounds, having poured oil and wine on them. Then he put him on his own animal, brought him to an inn, and took care of him. The next day he took out two denarii, gave them to the innkeeper, and said, 'Take care of him; and when I come back, I will repay you whatever more you spend. Which of these three, do you think, was a neighbor to the man who fell into the hands of the robbers?" He said, "The one who showed him mercy" Jesus said to him, "Go and do likewise."

3. Genesis 2:4b-3:24

In the day that the Lord God made the earth and the heavens, when no plant of the field was yet in the earth and no herb of the field had yet sprung up—for the Lord God had not caused it to rain upon the earth, and there was no one to till the ground; but a stream would rise from the earth, and water the whole face of the ground—then the Lord God formed man from the dust of the ground, and breathed into his nostrils the breath of life; and the man became a living being. And the Lord god planted a garden in Eden, in the east; and there he put the man whom he had formed. Out of the ground the Lord God made to grow every tree that is pleasant to the sight and good for food, the tree of life also in the midst of the garden, and the tree of the knowledge of good and evil.

A river flows out of Eden to water the garden, and from there it divides and becomes four branches. The name of the first is Pishon; it is the one that flows around the whole land of Havilah, where there is gold; and the gold of that land is good; bdellium and onyx stone are there. The name of the second river is Gihon; it is the one that flows around the whole land of Cush. The name of the third river is Tigris, which flows east of Assyria. And the fourth river is the Euphrates.

The Lord God took the man and put him in the garden of Eden to till it and keep it. And the Lord God commanded the man, "You may freely eat of every tree of the garden; but of the tree of the knowledge of good and evil you shall not eat, for in the day that you eat of it you shall die."

Then the Lord God said, "It is not good that the man should be alone; I will make him a helper as his partner." So out of the ground the Lord God formed every animal of the field and every bird of the air, and brought them to the man to see what he would call them; and whatever the man called every living creature, that was its name.

The man gave names to all cattle, and to the birds of the air, and to every animal of the field; but for the man there was not found a helper as his partner. So the Lord God caused a deep sleep to fall upon the man, and he slept; then he took one of his ribs and closed up its place with flesh. And the rib that the Lord God had taken from the man he made into a woman and brought her to the man. Then the man said,

"This at last is bone of my bones
　　and flesh of my flesh;
this one shall be called Woman,
　　for out of Man this one was taken."

Therefore a man leaves his father and his mother and clings to his wife, and they become one flesh. And the man and his wife were both naked, and were not ashamed.

Now the serpent was more crafty than any other wild animal that the Lord God had made. He said to the woman, "Did God say, 'You shall not eat from any tree in the garden'?" The woman said to the serpent, "We may eat of the fruit of the trees in the garden; but God said, 'You shall not eat of the fruit of the tree that is in the middle of the garden, nor shall you touch it, or you shall die.'" But the serpent said to the woman, "you will not die; for God knows that when you eat of it your eyes will be opened, and you will be like God, knowing good and evil." So when the woman saw that the tree was good for food, and that it was a delight to the eyes, and that the tree was to be desired to make one wise, she took of its fruit and ate; and she also gave some to her husband, who was with her, and he ate. Then the eyes of both were opened, and they knew that they were naked; and they sewed fig leaves together and made loincloths for themselves.

They heard the sound of the Lord God walking in the garden at the time of the evening breeze, and the man and his wife hid themselves from the presence of the Lord God among the trees of the garden. But the Lord God called to the man, and said to him, "Where are you?" He said, "I heard the sound of you in the garden, and I was afraid, because I was naked; and I hid myself." He said, "Who told you that you were naked? Have you eaten from the tree of which I commanded you not to eat?" The man said, "The woman whom you gave to be with me, she gave me fruit from the tree, and I ate."

Then the Lord God said to the woman, "What is this that you have done?" The woman said, "The serpent tricked me, and I ate." The Lord God said to the serpent,

"Because you have done this,
cursed are you among all animals
and among all wild creatures;
upon your belly you shall go,
and dust you shall eat
all the days of your life.
I will put enmity between you and the woman,
and between your offspring and hers;
he will strike your head,
and you will strike his heel."

To the woman he said,

"I will greatly increase your pangs in
childbearing;
in pain you shall bring forth children,
yet your desire shall be for your husband,
and he shall rule over you."

And to the man he said,

"Because you have listened to the voice
of your wife,

and have eaten of the tree
about which I commanded you,
'You shall not eat of it,'
cursed is the ground because of you;
in toil you shall eat of it all the days
of your life;
thorns and thistles it shall bring forth
for you;
and you shall eat the plants of the
field.
By the sweat of your face
you shall eat bread
until you return to the ground,
for out of it you were taken;
you are dust,
and to dust you shall return."

The man named his wife Eve, because she was the mother of all living. And the Lord God made garments of skins for the man and for his wife, and clothed them.

Then the Lord God said, "See, the man has become like one of us, knowing good and evil; and now, he might reach out his hand and take also from the tree of life, and eat, and live forever"—therefore the Lord God sent him forth from the garden of Eden, to till the ground from which he was taken. He drove out the man; and at the east of the garden of Eden he placed the cherubim and a sword flaming and turning to guard the way to the tree of life.

4. John 4:6-30

Jacob's well was there, and Jesus, tired out by his journey, was sitting by the well. It was about noon.

A Samaritan woman came to draw water, and Jesus said to her, "Give me a drink." (His disciples had gone to the city to buy food.) The Samaritan woman said to him, "How is it that you, a Jew, ask a drink of me, a woman of Samaria?" (Jews do not share things in common with Samaritans.) Jesus answered her, "If you knew the gift of

God, and who it is that is saying to you, 'Give me a drink,' you would have asked him, and he would have given you living water." The woman said to him, "Sir, you have no bucket, and the well is deep. Where do you get that living water? Are you greater than our ancestor Jacob, who gave us the well, and with his sons and his flocks drank from it?" Jesus said to her, "Everyone who drinks of this water will be thirsty again, but those who drink of the water that I will give them will never be thirsty. The water that I will give will become in them a spring of water gushing up to eternal life." The woman said to him, "Sir, give me this water, so that I may never be thirsty or have to keep coming here to draw water."

Jesus said to her, "Go, call your husband, and come back." The woman answered him, "I have no husband." Jesus said to her, "You are right in saying, 'I have no husband'; for you have had five husbands, and the one you have now is not your husband. What you have said is true!" The woman said to him, "Sir, I see that you are a prophet. Our ancestors worshiped on this mountain, but you say that the place where people must worship is in Jerusalem." Jesus said to her, "Woman, believe me, the hour is coming when you will worship the Father neither on this mountain nor in Jerusalem. You worship what you do not know; we worship what we know, for salvation is from the Jews. But the hour is coming and is now here, when the true worshipers will worship the Father in spirit and truth, for the Father seeks such as these to worship him. God is spirit, and those who worship him must worship in spirit and truth." The woman said to him, "I know that Messiah is coming" (who is called Christ). "When he comes, he will proclaim all things to us." Jesus said to her, "I am he, the one who is speaking to you."

Just then his disciples came. They were astonished that he was speaking with a woman, but no one said, "What do you want?" or, "Why are you speaking with her?"

Then the woman left her water jar and went back to the city. She said to the people, "Come and see a man who told me everything I have ever done! He cannot be the Messiah, can he?" They left the city and were on their way to him.

5. Matthew 9:9-13

As Jesus was walking along, he saw a man called Matthew sitting at the tax booth; and he said to him, "Follow me." And he got up and followed him.

And as he sat at dinner in the house, many tax collectors and sinners came and were sitting with him and his disciples. When the Pharisees saw this, they said to his disciples, "Why does your teacher eat with tax collectors and sinners?" But when he heard this, he said, "Those who are well have no need of a physician, but those who are sick. Go and learn what this means, 'I desire mercy, not sacrifice.' For I have come to call not the righteous but sinners."

Luke 5:27-32

After this he went out and saw a tax collector named Levi, sitting at the tax booth, and he said to him, "Follow me." And he got up, left everything, and followed him.

Then Levi gave a great banquet for him in his house; and there was a large crowd of tax collectors and others sitting at the table with them. The Pharisees and their scribes were complaining to his disciples, saying, "Why do you eat and drink with tax collectors and sinners?" Jesus answered, "Those who are well have no need of a physician, but those who are sick; I have come to call not the righteous but sinners to repentance."

Mark 2:13-17

Jesus went out again beside the sea; the whole crowd gathered around him, and he taught them. As he was walking along, he saw Levi son of Alphaeus sitting at the tax booth, and he said to him, "Follow me." And he got up and followed him.

And as he sat at dinner in Levi's house, many tax collectors and sinners were also sitting with Jesus and his disciples—for there were many who followed him. When the scribes of the Pharisees saw that he was eating with sinners and tax collectors, they said to his disciples, "Why does he eat with tax collectors and sinners?" When Jesus heard this, he said to them, "Those who are well have no need of a physician, but those who are sick; I have come to call not the righteous but sinners."

6. Luke 19:1-10

He entered Jericho and was passing through it. A man was there named Zacchaeus; he was a chief tax collector and was rich. He was trying to see who Jesus was, but on account of the crowd he could not, because he was short in stature. So he ran ahead and climbed a sycamore tree to see him, because he was gong to pass that way. When Jesus came to the place, he looked up and said to him, "Zacchaeus, hurry and come down; for I must stay at your house today." So he hurried down and was happy to welcome him. All who saw it began to grumble and said, "He has gone to be the guest of one who is a sinner." Zacchaeus stood there and said to the Lord, "Look, half of my possessions, Lord, I will give to the poor; and if I have defrauded anyone of anything, I will pay back four times as much." Then Jesus said to him, "Today salvation has come to this house, because he too is a son of Abraham. For the Son of Man came to seek out and to save the lost."

7. Matthew 8:1-4

When Jesus had come down from the mountain, great crowds followed him; and there was a leper who came to him and knelt before him, saying, "Lord, if you choose, you can make me clean." He stretched out his hand and touched him, saying, "I do choose. Be made clean!"

Immediately his leprosy was cleansed. Then Jesus said to him, "See that you say nothing to anyone; but go, show yourself to the priest, and offer the gift that Moses commanded, as a testimony to them."

Mark 1:40-47

A leper came to him begging him, and kneeling, he said to him, "If you choose, you can make me clean." Moved with pity, Jesus stretched out his hand and touched him, and said to him, "I do choose. Be made clean!" Immediately the leprosy left him, and he was made clean. After sternly warning him he sent him away at once, saying to him, "See that you say nothing to anyone; but go, show yourself to the priest, and offer for your cleansing what Moses commanded, as a testimony to them." But he went out and began to proclaim it freely, and to spread the word, so that Jesus could no longer go into a town openly, but stayed out in the country; and people came to him from every quarter.

Luke 5:12-16

Once, when he was in one of the cities, there was a man covered with leprosy. When he saw Jesus, he bowed with his face to the ground and begged him, "Lord, if you choose, you can make me clean." Then Jesus stretched out his hand, touched him, and said, "I do choose. Be made clean." Immediately the leprosy left him. And he ordered him to tell no one. "Go," he said, "and show yourself to the priest, and, as Moses commanded, make an offering for your cleansing, for a testimony to them." But now more than ever the word about Jesus spread abroad; many crowds would gather to hear him and to be cured of their diseases. But he would withdraw to deserted places and pray.

8. John 8:1-11

Then each of them went home, while Jesus went to the Mount of Olives. Early in the morning he came again to the temple. All the people came to him and he sat down and began to teach them. The scribes and the Pharisees brought a woman who had been caught in adultery; and making her stand before all of them, they said to him, “Teacher, this woman was caught in the very act of committing adultery. Now in the law Moses commanded us to stone such women. Now what do you say?” They said this to test him, so that they might have some charge to bring against him. Jesus bent down and wrote with his finger on the ground. When they kept on questioning him, he straightened up and said to them, “Let anyone among you who is without sin be the first to throw a stone at her.” And once again he bent down and wrote on the ground. When they heard it, they went away, one by one, beginning with the elders; and Jesus was left alone with the woman standing before him. Jesus straightened up and said to her, “Woman, where are they? Has no one condemned you?” She said, “No one, sir.” And Jesus said, “Neither do I condemn you. Go your way, and from now on do not sin again.”

9. Matthew 9:1-8

And after getting into a boat he crossed the sea and came to his own town.

And just then some people were carrying a paralyzed man lying on a bed. When Jesus saw their faith, he said to the paralytic, “Take heart, son, your sins are forgiven.” Then some of the scribes said to themselves, “This man is blaspheming.” But Jesus, perceiving their thoughts, said, “Why do you think evil in your hearts? For which is easier, to say, ‘Your sins are forgiven,’ or to say, ‘Stand up and walk’? But so that you may know that the Son of Man has authority on earth to forgive sins”—he then said to the paralytic—“Stand up, take your bed and go to your home.” And he stood up and went to his home. When the crowds saw it, they were filled with awe, and they glorified God, who had given such authority to human beings.

Mark 2:1-12

When he returned to Capernaum after some days, it was reported that he was at home. So many gathered around that there was no longer room for them, not even in front of the door; and he was speaking the word to them. Then some people came, bringing to him a paralyzed man, carried by four of them. And when they could not bring him to Jesus because of the crowd, they removed the roof above him; and after having dug through it, they let down the mat on which the paralytic lay. When Jesus saw their faith, he said to the paralytic, "Son, your sins are forgiven." Now some of the scribes were sitting there, questioning in their hearts, "Why does this fellow speak in this way? It is blasphemy! Who can forgive sins but God alone?" At once Jesus perceived in his spirit that they were discussing these questions among themselves; and he said to them, "Why do you raise such questions in your hearts? Which is easier to say to the paralytic, 'Your sins are forgiven,' or to say 'Stand up and take your mat and walk'? But so that you may know that the Son of Man has authority on earth to forgive sins"—he said to the paralytic—"I say to you, stand up, take your mat and go to your home." And he stood up, and immediately took the mat and went out before all of them; so that they were all amazed and glorified God, saying, "We have never seen anything like this!"

Luke 5:17-26

One day, while he was teaching, Pharisees and teachers of the law were sitting nearby (they had come from every village of Galilee and Judea and from Jerusalem); and the power of the Lord was with him to heal. Just then some men came, carrying a paralyzed man on a bed. They were trying to bring him in and lay him before Jesus; but finding no way to bring him in because of the crowd, they went up on the roof and let him down with his bed through the tiles into the middle of the crowd in front of Jesus When he saw their faith, he said, "Friend, your sins are forgiven you." Then the scribes and the Pharisees began to question, "Who is this who is speaking blasphemies? Who can forgive sins but God alone?" When Jesus perceived their questionings, he answered them, "Why do you raise such questions in your hearts? Which is easier, to say, 'Your sins are forgiven you,' or to say 'Stand up and walk'? But so that you may know that the Son of Man has authority on earth to forgive sins"—he said to the one who was paralyzed—"I say to you, stand up and take your bed and go to your home." Immediately he stood up before them, took what he had been lying on, and went to his home, glorifying God. Amazement seized all of them, and they glorified God and were filled with awe, saying, "We have seen strange things today."

10. Matthew 18:21-22

Then Peter came and said to him, "Lord, if another member of the church sins against me, how often should I forgive? As many as seven times?" Jesus said to him, "Not seven times, but I tell you, seventy-seven times."

Luke 17:4

"And if the same person sins against you seven times a day, and turns back to you seven times and says, 'I repent,' you must forgive."

11. Matthew 18:23-35

"For this reason the kingdom of heaven may be compared to a king who wished to settle accounts with his slaves. When he began the reckoning, one who owed him ten thousand talents was brought to him; and, as he could not pay, his lord ordered him to be sold, together with his wife and children and all his possessions, and payment to be made. So the slave fell on his knees before him, saying, 'Have patience with me, and I will pay you everything.' And out of pity for him the lord of that slave released him and forgave him the debt. But that same slave, as he went out, came upon one of his fellow slaves who owed him a hundred denarii; and seizing him by the throat, he said, 'Pay what you owe.' Then his fellow slave fell down and pleaded with him, 'Have patience with me, and I will pay you.' But he refused; then he went and threw him into prison until he would pay the debt. When his fellow slaves saw what had happened, they were greatly distressed, and they went and reported to their lord all that had taken place. Then his lord summoned him and said to him, 'You wicked slave! I forgave you all that debt because you pleaded with me. Should you not have had mercy on your fellow slave, as I had mercy on you?' And in anger his lord handed him over to be tortured until he would pay his entire debt. So my heavenly Father will also do to every one of you, if you do not forgive your brother or sister from your heart."

12. I Corinthians 13:1-13 (See Chapter 3, #15)

13. Matthew 25:31-46

"When the Son of Man comes in his glory, and all the angels with him, then he will sit on the throne of his glory. All the nations will be gathered before him, and he will separate people one from another as a shepherd separates the sheep from the goats, and he will put the sheep at his right hand and the goats at the left. Then, the king will say to those at his right hand, 'Come, you that are blessed by my Father, inherit the kingdom prepared for you from the foundation of the world; for I was hungry and you gave me food, I was thirsty and you gave me something to drink, I was a stranger and you welcomed me. I was naked and you gave me clothing, I was sick and you took care of me, I was in prison and you visited me.' Then the righteous will answer him, 'Lord when was it that we saw you hungry and gave you food, or thirsty and gave you something to drink? And when was it that we saw you a stranger and welcomed you, or naked and gave you clothing? And when was it that we saw you sick or in prison and visited you?' And the king will answer them, 'Truly I tell you, just as you did it to one of the least of these who are members of my family, you did it to me.' Then he will say to those at his left hand, 'You that are accursed, depart from me into the eternal fire prepared for the devil and his angels; for I was hungry and you gave me no food, I was thirsty and you gave me nothing to drink, I was a stranger and you did not welcome me, naked and you did not give me clothing, sick and in prison and you did not visit me.' Then they also will answer, "Lord, when was it that we saw you hungry or thirsty or a stranger or naked or sick or in prison, and did not take care of you?' Then he will answer them, 'Truly I tell you, just as you did not do it to one of the least of these, you did not do it to me.' And these will go away into eternal punishment, but the righteous into eternal life."

Chapter 7, ***PUTTING THE ETHICS OF JESUS INTO ACTION***

1. Luke 4:16-30 (See Chapter 3, #17)

2. Luke 6:1-11

   One Sabbath while Jesus was going through the grainfields, his disciples plucked some heads of grain, rubbed them in their hands, and ate them. But some of the Pharisees said, "Why are you doing what is not lawful on the Sabbath?" Jesus answered, "Have you not read what David did when he and his companions were hungry? He entered the house of God and took and ate the bread of the Presence, which it is not lawful for any but the priests to eat, and gave some to his companions?" Then he said to them, "The Son of Man is lord of the Sabbath."

On another Sabbath he entered the synagogue and taught, and there was a man there whose right hand was withered. The scribes and the Pharisees watched him to see whether he would cure on the Sabbath, so that they might find an accusation against him. Even though he knew what they were thinking, he said to the man who had the withered hand, "Come and stand here." He got up and stood there. Then Jesus said to them, "I ask you, is it lawful to do good or to do harm on the Sabbath, to save life or to destroy it?" After looking around at all of them, he said to him, "Stretch out your hand." He did so, and his hand was restored. But they were filled with fury and discussed with one another what they might do to Jesus.

3. Luke 2:48

   When his parents saw him they were astonished; and his mother said to him, "Child, why have you treated us like this? Look, your father and I have been searching for you in great anxiety."

   John 1:45

   Philip found Nathanael and said to him, "We have found him about whom Moses in the law and also the prophets wrote, Jesus son of Joseph from Nazareth."

4. Matthew 23:1-39 (See Chapter 3 #16)

5. Matthew 9:1-8

   And after getting into a boat he crossed the sea and came to his own town.

   And just then some people were carrying a paralyzed man lying on a bed. When Jesus saw their faith, he said to the paralytic, "Take heart, son, your sins are forgiven." Then some of the scribes said to themselves, "This man is blaspheming." But Jesus, perceiving their thoughts, said, "Why do you think evil in your hearts? For which is easier, to say, 'Your sins are forgiven,' or to say, 'Stand up and walk'? But so that you may know that the Son of Man has authority on earth to forgive sins"—he then said to the paralytic—"Stand up, take your bed and go to your home." And he stood up and went to his home. When the crowds saw it, they were filled with awe, and they glorified God, who had given such authority to human beings.